Best wishes on your
measurment journey!

—Josh Belur,

About This Book

Why is this topic important?

Corporate training makes up one of the largest discretionary expenditures in organizations. Organizations spend as much as 3 to 4 percent of payroll on this important area, yet few are able to adequately measure its effectiveness, efficiency, and impact.

How can executives and training professionals more easily measure these investments in a way that provides actionable and credible information? How can they free themselves from the traditional approaches of Kirkpatrick and Phillips to implement pragmatic, useful, and easy-to-implement approaches to the measurement of training?

What will you achieve from this book?

This book, developed after more than five years of research, answers these questions. It provides an easy-to-follow, business-driven, pragmatic approach to training measurement that has been developed through research with hundreds of organizations. "The Impact Measurement Framework®" provides a complete solution to help training managers and executives develop and implement a complete measurement program.

How is this book organized?

The Training Measurement Book is organized into five major sections: First, the general principles of training measurement—why and how should we measure training? What are the pros and cons of using ROI? What are the limitations of the Kirkpatrick model? How do we provide measurement programs that are actionable and credible? Second, the book discusses the Impact Measurement Framework®, and the nine measurement areas important to a total measurement program. Third, the book details the seven-step training measurement process, identifying best practices, tips, and techniques that make training measurement easy. Fourth, the book discusses the use of tools, technologies, and systems that can make training measurement more efficient. And finally, the book includes in-depth case studies, examples, and an in-depth discussion of the topic of training analytics, to help the reader understand how organizations have implemented pragmatic, actionable, and efficient measurement programs.

About Pfeiffer

Pfeiffer serves the professional development and hands-on resource needs of training and human resource practitioners and gives them products to do their jobs better. We deliver proven ideas and solutions from experts in HR development and HR management, and we offer effective and customizable tools to improve workplace performance. From novice to seasoned professional, Pfeiffer is the source you can trust to make yourself and your organization more successful.

Essential Knowledge Pfeiffer produces insightful, practical, and comprehensive materials on topics that matter the most to training and HR professionals. Our Essential Knowledge resources translate the expertise of seasoned professionals into practical, how-to guidance on critical workplace issues and problems. These resources are supported by case studies, worksheets, and job aids and are frequently supplemented with CD-ROMs, websites, and other means of making the content easier to read, understand, and use.

Essential Tools Pfeiffer's Essential Tools resources save time and expense by offering proven, ready-to-use materials—including exercises, activities, games, instruments, and assessments—for use during a training or team-learning event. These resources are frequently offered in looseleaf or CD-ROM format to facilitate copying and customization of the material.

Pfeiffer also recognizes the remarkable power of new technologies in expanding the reach and effectiveness of training. While e-hype has often created whizbang solutions in search of a problem, we are dedicated to bringing convenience and enhancements to proven training solutions. All our e-tools comply with rigorous functionality standards. The most appropriate technology wrapped around essential content yields the perfect solution for today's on-the-go trainers and human resource professionals.

Pfeiffer
www.pfeiffer.com

Essential resources for training and HR professionals

The Training Measurement Book

Best Practices, Proven Methodologies, and Practical Approaches

Featuring "The Impact Measurement Framework®": A Business-Driven Approach to the Measurement of Corporate Learning

Josh Bersin

A Wiley Imprint
www.pfeiffer.com

Published by Pfeiffer
An Imprint of Wiley
989 Market Street, San Francisco, CA 94103-1741   www.pfeiffer.com

For additional copies/bulk purchases of this book in the U.S. please contact 800-274-4434.

Pfeiffer books and products are available through most bookstores. To contact Pfeiffer directly call our Customer Care Department within the U.S. at 800-274-4434, outside the U.S. at 317-572-3985, fax 317-572-4002, or visit www.pfeiffer.com.

Pfeiffer also publishes its books in a variety of electronic formats. Some content that appears in print may not be available in electronic books.

Library of Congress Cataloging-in-Publication Data
Bersin, Josh.
    The training measurement book: best practices, proven methodologies, and practical approaches / Josh Bersin.
        p.cm.
    "Featuring The impact measurement framework: a business-driven approach to the measurement of corporate learning." Includes bibliographical references and index.
    ISBN 978-0-7879-7544-9 (cloth)
        1. Employees—Training of—Evaluation. 2. Employees—Training of—Evaluation— Case studies. 3. Organizational learning. 4. Organizational learning—Case studies. I. Title.
HF5549.5.T7B4816 2008
658.3'124—dc22
                                                                            2007049554

Acquiring Editor: Lisa Shannon   Editor: Rebecca Taff
Director of Development: Kathleen Dolan Davies   Editorial Assistant: Marisa Kelley
Developmental Editor: Leslie Stephen   Manufacturing Supervisor: Becky Morgan
Production Editor: Dawn Kilgore

Printed in the United States of America

Printing   10 9 8 7 6 5 4 3 2 1

Contents

Introduction

The Challenge of Training Measurement

One of the most difficult challenges in corporate training is measurement. How can learning and development managers best measure the effectiveness and efficiency of training programs? How can training leaders monitor program alignment and contribution to overall business goals? How can senior management obtain consistent information about the training function to help tune and optimize the organization? And how can line of business managers understand the value of training their people?

Our research over the last several years indicates that measurement of corporate training continues to be a profound challenge for most organizations. In 2005, 2006, and 2007, we surveyed our research readers (more than six hundred senior and mid-level training managers) and asked them to select their top two challenges for the coming year. In every year, more than 90 percent rated measurement as the number one or number two area they would like to improve. Senior executives are even more concerned. In 2007, we asked more than seven hundred HR and learning executives how well their learning programs were aligned with their organizations' talent needs. Surprisingly, only 4 percent rated their organizations as "fully aligned" and only 15 percent rated themselves as "well aligned" with the organization's most critical talent needs.[1]

When we conducted a survey of 136 training executives to understand their level of maturity in managing and measuring the training process, we found an astounding lack of sophistication.[2] While 74 percent of organizations believe that it is important to measure the job impact of training programs, only 14 percent actually do. And 72 percent of learning executives believe that it is extremely important to measure the business impact of training—while only 10 percent have any such measurement program in place. And most surprising of all, when we asked training executives whether they had a written business plan for learning that establishes measurable goals and objectives, only 52 percent said yes.

These results are particularly surprising, considering the fact that U.S. corporations spend more than $55 billion on training and there are more than three hundred books and articles discussing the topic. It is clear that continuous new approaches are needed.

I run an organization that studies trends, best practices, and benchmarks in corporate training and HR organizations. Prior to this career, I spent more than seven years in the field of data warehousing and business intelligence. During that time I spoke with hundreds of companies that had built highly sophisticated measurement processes for marketing, sales, and other business functions. In these disciplines, managers also struggle to measure intangibles—but they have implemented many well-established, business-relevant solutions.

In my research into the measurement of corporate learning and HR, I found a highly complex problem. There are so many things to measure: financial measures, operational measures, effectiveness, alignment, and impact on the business itself. As with operations like marketing and IT, training does not directly contribute to the bottom line, so all measures are "indirect" in some way. And despite a wide acceptance of existing models, practitioners continue to be frustrated.

During this research I identified a wide variety of best-practice solutions that really work (and a large number of anxious organizations that want desperately to improve their measurement programs). Although the problem of measuring training initially seems very complex, over time it has become clear to me that the basic principles to a sound measurement program are actually very simple.

The goal of this book is to try to clarify and simply this topic, providing the reader with many easy ways to implement a training measurement program. I will explain specific best practices we identified through our WhatWorks® research process.[3] This research process focuses on identifying pragmatic, actionable, specific best practices, processes, and methodologies that most organizations can immediately use. Also, because this area is so complex, I have taken the liberty of providing "advice" or "opinions" based on my personal assessment of approaches that did not work and may cause problems.

Readers of this book are encouraged to contact me with any comments regarding this research—your feedback and comments are an integral part of the ongoing quest to make learning and learning measurement more effective, efficient, and business-aligned.

Need for New Measurement Models

As I embarked on this process I realized that I was entering a world of giants: Donald Kirkpatrick and Jack Phillips. While I greatly respect them as creative, innovative thinkers in our industry, I found that their well-known models were often holding organizations back.

How did I come to such a conclusion? We have examined the maturity of training measurement for many years. In 2004 and then again in 2006 we examined organizations' progress in the area of measurement. What we found was astounding: the percent of organizations measuring the ROI, job impact, and business impact of training is flat to declining.[4] My anecdotal conversations with training managers and executives support this finding: most feel frustrated that their measurement programs are lacking.

This is a problem organizations spend between 1 to 4 percent of their entire payroll on training ($55 billion in 2006 in the United States alone[5]), yet the majority of large and small organizations continue to have challenges with the process of measuring its effectiveness, impact, and efficiency. If we are going to continue to drive business impact from our training programs, we must address the problem of operational measurement.

So why does training measurement continue to be so difficult? First, of course, training is a very "intangible" process, so any approach to measuring its impact is imperfect. We address this problem in this book by moving beyond "impact" to many other important, actionable measures. Second, I believe many organizations are held back by the limitations of the existing well-known measurement models, primarily the Kirkpatrick[6] model. The Kirkpatrick model describes four levels for measurement: learner satisfaction (reaction), learning, job impact (behavior), and business impact (results). Return on Investment (ROI) is often called a fifth level—and ROI measurement has been well defined and popularized by Jack Phillips.[7]

While these models are widely understood and have done much to help training managers understand and improve measurement programs, they limit an organization's thinking and make the measurement process difficult to implement. In fact, our research shows that only 4 to 5 percent of organizations measure ROI (and they do so for a very small percentage of their programs), and fewer than 10 percent regularly measure business impact. I cannot even count the number of times a training manager has started the training measurement conversation with the question "How do I measure level 3?" My answer: You may not have to. Practitioners need a more pragmatic, business-oriented approach.

As I learned about other pragmatic and workable approaches, I found it necessary to summarize my findings into a framework. This framework, which I call the Impact Measurement Framework®, pulls together all the best practices I learned into a complete "thought model" for training measurement. Yes, it is another model—but rather than try to memorize it as a whole, I hope you can use the elements of it that apply to your particular organization.

This framework extends the Kirkpatrick model in several ways.

- First, it goes beyond the concept of measuring training programs and addresses the issues of measuring the training operation itself. It is important for training managers to realize that they exist in a corporate organization and that they must measure the effectiveness, efficiency, and alignment of their entire operation and operational processes.

- Second, in order to help understand how to measure impact, the framework proposes a causal model that answers the general question "How does training actually drive business results?" This "impact model" is simple and easy to understand and gives training managers and executives a set of easy-to-understand causal elements to consider measuring. If you believe the impact model is correct, then you will immediately see some new things to measure.

- Third, the framework identifies nine specific measurement areas that can be used to monitor and evaluate each of these causal elements. These measurement areas extend the Kirkpatrick model significantly and build on many of Kirkpatrick's principles. Organizations can select one or more of these nine measures to monitor and evaluate their training programs, depending on their maturity level and business environment. You do not need to "buy off" on the entire framework to gain a lot of value.

- Fourth, the framework was developed with full knowledge of today's complex training programs—programs that include e-learning, coaching, collaboration, on-the-job exercises, podcasts, and a wide variety of blended learning elements.

In addition to the framework, throughout the book I have included many specific examples and best practices to show you how to apply the framework to your particular environment. So rather than promote the framework itself, the book is designed to give you many good ideas and practical examples you can immediately apply.

I have presented the framework to many training managers, and most find that it is easy to understand, business-oriented, and actionable. They often feel alarmed that it is different from the traditional Kirkpatrick approach. Please do not feel threatened in any way: the framework extends Kirkpatrick's thinking and should give you new ideas that do not replace or eliminate any of the processes you are currently using. Ultimately, I hope that it gives you a sense of clarity and freedom to implement a repeatable process that fits your organization's business needs.

Structure of This Book

This book is structured as follows to enable readers to find the most appropriate information.

General Principles of Training Measurement. This chapter serves as the executive overview of the findings and best practices. These principles are universal and can be applied to any organization attempting to build a measurement program.

The Pros and Cons of Using ROI. This chapter discusses the pros and cons of using ROI in training measurement, a topic we believe has been over-promoted in training measurement. It gives our perspectives of where and when to use ROI approaches for greatest impact.

Limitations of the Kirkpatrick Model. This chapter reviews the Kirkpatrick model and where it fits. It discusses some of its limitations and why organizations should strive to move "beyond Kirkpatrick" in their thinking about business-oriented measurement program.

The Impact Measurement Framework. In this chapter, I explain the Business Impact Model® and Impact Measurement Framework®. I identify nine major measurement areas that can be used for training measurement and tie these nine areas back to the causal model for training impact, making it easy to decide where one wants to focus in the measurement of impact.

Implementation: The Seven-Step Training Measurement Process. In this chapter I walk the reader through the seven-step measurement process. Although most organizations will not use all seven steps, seeing these steps tied together will enable you to understand how to apply them to the implementation of a complete program. This section includes many examples and best practices for each step.

Measurement of Business Impact. This chapter specifically addresses the important and difficult question of how to measure the business impact from training. Several approaches are described, and best practices and examples are given.

Measurement of Alignment. Alignment is one of the nine measurement areas in the Impact Measurement Framework. This chapter specifically explains what alignment means, as well as how organizations can measure and improve business alignment. Detailed examples are provided of how several organizations (Caterpillar, CNA, Motorola, and others) use their planning processes to drive, measure, and monitor business alignment.

Attainment: Measurement of Customer Satisfaction. One of the nine measurement areas in this book is attainment of customer satisfaction. Since this is a new topic in training measurement, this chapter specifically details this subject and how several organizations use customer satisfaction as an important measurement area. It also explains how Six Sigma measurement approaches can be applied to the training function.

Measurement Tools and Technologies. In this chapter we review some of the key tools and technologies for training measurement. Without attempting to review or discuss every measurement tool on the market, we highlight the role of the learning management system, along with some particular tools that greatly aid the measurement process.

The Journey Forward: Focus on What Matters. In this chapter we discuss the roadmap to building a broadly deployed measurement program. The measurement process is not an end in itself—but rather, a journey. In this section, we explain where to start and how your company's measurement program will evolve over time.

Appendices I and II: Case Studies A and B. Two important case studies are included here: Randstad and HP. Case Study A: *Randstad Measures Onboarding* covers the processes and techniques that this company (a very successful international staffing agency) uses for onboarding new employees. Case Study B: *HP Develops an Integrated Measurement Process* covers this company's journey from an ad-hoc measurement process to a formalized and structured, enterprise-wide measurement process for training. Both case studies provide best practices and approaches that can be applied to any organization.

Appendix III: Research: The State of Training Measurement Today. This section includes the results of this industry survey of 136 training executives and managers, illustrating the current state of their training measurement processes, operational plans, technologies, and desires.

Appendix IV: Examples of Learning Measurements. In this section, we include a variety of measurement snapshots from Caterpillar, DAU, Cisco, Microsoft, and others that show how these organizations measure, display, and manage their training functions.

Appendix V: Specific Learning Measures. This section details sample measures that can be implemented, based on the Business Impact Measurement Framework.

Appendix VI: Training Analytics Specifications. More and more organizations are deciding that part of their measurement initiative is the purchase or development of a system for training analytics. The section describes the specifications and business requirements for a learning analytics system. This appendix provides the details, which will be helpful in building, selecting, and understanding how such a system can help a learning organization manage and automate the measurement process.

Methodology for This Research

The research for this book spans many hundreds of organizations over the last five years. In particular, more than two hundred different organizations have been interviewed to discuss their measurement programs, tools, design strategies, and implementation experiences. Training measurement strategies and challenges have been discussed in workshops with hundreds of training directors and managers, as well. In addition, three major research surveys have been conducted (targeting training managers and executives) to better understand the trends, implementation experiences, and strategies. More than 1,700 responses to these three surveys have been received, mostly from organizations in North America. You can read more about the detailed research in Appendix III.

Some of the companies that provided valuable case studies and examples include the following: *Caterpillar, Children's Hospital of Philadelphia, Defense Acquisition University, Depository Trust & Clearing Corp., Eaton, EDS, FedExKinko's, HP, KPMG Canada, McDonald's, Northwest Airlines, Pep Boys, Randstad, Saks Fifth Avenue, Sprint, Wells Fargo, and Wendy's.*

Vendors that have provided valuable insights into this book include: *KnowledgeAdvisors, NIIT/Cognitive Arts, Plateau, Saba, SumTotal Systems, and Zero'd In Technologies*

A Personal Comment

Our clients and research members continuously tell us that their biggest challenge in corporate learning is the implementation of a robust measurement program.

As we interviewed program managers and executives, we found that many had implemented very innovative and powerful ideas. These ideas were pragmatic, easy to implement, and highly actionable. We became excited about the simple and powerful approaches organizations are taking.

Organizations approach measurement in different ways. I have talked with organizations that try to implement scientific studies of in-depth job impact; I have talked with organizations that analyze thousands of data elements in statistical detail: and I have talked with organizations that focus on only a few major scorecard elements to drive success.

We need to accept the fact that the measurement of training impact is difficult because we are trying to measure factors that drive human performance. As we all know well, human performance is driven by a wide variety of factors, including skills, knowledge, attitude, environment, experience, health, organizational culture, management, and business environment. To be successful I believe it is important to simplify the problem and measure things that are both easy to measure and highly actionable. In many cases the most valuable measures organizations capture are what we call "indicators"—easily measured things that are indicators of performance and outcomes. These indicators are much easier to measure than performance and outcomes themselves. "Satisfaction" is actually one of these indicators.

Ultimately, by starting small and implementing a repeatable and scalable process, organizations can develop highly actionable measurements quickly. Over time, these processes can grow, become more sophisticated, and adapt to meet more business needs. I hope that this book helps managers identify these easy-to-implement approaches and demystify the training measurement process so that more people will begin this journey.

Notes

1. For more information, *High-Impact Talent Management: Trends, Best Practices, and Industry Solutions*. Bersin & Associates/Josh Bersin, May 2007. Available at www.bersin.com.
2. See Appendix III for details.
3. Bersin & Associates' *WhatWorks*® Research Methodology is continuous, in-depth research into the enterprise learning and performance management marketplace. For more information, please visit: www.bersin.com.
4. See Appendix III for details on this survey.
5. For more information, *The Corporate Learning Factbook*® *2007: Statistics, Benchmarks and Analysis of the U.S. Corporate Training Market*. Bersin & Associates/Karen O'Leonard, February 2007. Available at www.bersin.com.
6. Donald Kirkpatrick's four-level measurement model has been widely published in many articles and its terminology is well-known to most training professionals. The original model was published in R.L. Craig's *Training and Development Handbook*. New York: McGraw-Hill, 1976.
7. For more information, see *The Handbook of Training Evaluation and Measurement Methods*. Houston, TX: Gulf Publishing, 1991. (Jack Phillips' ROI, or "fifth level," was first published in this book.)

Chapter One

General Principles of Training Measurement

The first step in this complex topic is to set some ground rules. In this section we will discuss some basic principles that summarize our general findings and recommendations about training measurement. You should consider these principles as guidelines throughout your training measurement journey.

1. Measurement Should Deliver Actionable Information

Before you start to figure out what to measure, you should ask yourself a more fundamental question: why? Why are we measuring training? What is the real purpose? Let me propose an answer:

The purpose of measuring any business process is to obtain *actionable information for improvement.*

In any business or operational function, measurement is a tool for improvement. It exists for one and only one purpose: to give you specific information you can act upon. Consider the dashboard of your car. It includes highly actionable information: speed, amount of gas, water temperature, number of miles driven, and whether the lights are on or not. You can glance at your dashboard and decide what to do. You should "slow down," or "get gas," or "put water in the radiator." These measures are not particularly high level or exciting, but they are really important and really actionable.

Consider what your dashboard does not include: it does not include the "current market value of your car" or "how good a deal you got at the dealer." This information, which may make you feel good (or bad), is not actionable. (I would argue that in many cases ROI is one of these.)

Now consider what information about training would be highly actionable. Let us look at measurement areas and the actions we could take based on good measurements:

Program Effectiveness and Alignment. How can continuous improvements be made to the programs, processes, and organization to become more effective and aligned with the business? Did the line managers support this program? Did they have enough input? Did we communicate its goal and structure effectively? Did we market and support it well? Is the program current and topical, given the critical operational issues we face today?

Program Design and Delivery. Which elements in a program work well and which do not? How does our delivery model work well, and where can we improve it? Which instructors or facilities are performing well or poorly? Who in our target audience found it valuable and why? Who did not find it useful and why? Which elements of our e-learning were effective and which were not?

Program Efficiency. How well are we utilizing our financial and human resources? Are we delivering training programs at the lowest possible cost per student-hour? How does the cost per hour of program A compare to the cost per hour of program B? Is it worth the extra cost or not? Are we leveraging e-learning in a cost-effective way? Where can we save money and create higher value for lower cost? How can we continuously drive down the cost of content development and delivery?

Operational Effectiveness. How well are we contributing to our organization's strategic goals? How well are we meeting our operational business plan[1] for learning? Where can we improve our time-to-market, attainment of our training objectives, and alignment with other HR or talent initiatives?

Compliance. If this training is mandatory, who is in compliance and who is out of compliance? What manager or workgroups are out of compliance? When do people have to recertify themselves? What elements of the program have caused any compliance issues? Did we reach our target audience or not? Why not?

Larger Talent Challenges. How well are line-of-business managers completing their training goals? Are compliance programs being met and, if not, why not? How well is training meeting the needs of performance planning and development planning? Are your programs meeting the organization's needs for skills gaps and strategic development?

These are important questions. In essence, your goal in measurement should be to obtain information that "operationalizes" your training function and gives you, the HR organization, and line-of-business managers the information needed to take action.

Defining the Term "Actionable Information"

Let us define the term. "Actionable information" refers to information that can be used to make specific business decisions. For example: Did the simulation program we developed drive the right level of learning? Should we have had more prerequisites? How cost-effective was this program versus others we delivered? Which components should be kept and which should be discarded? For which audience groups was it appropriate? Which audience groups did not find this program appropriate, and why?

Actionable information can be used to make specific business decisions. Actionable information has three key attributes:

1. Actionable Information Is Specific. To be actionable, the information or data we obtain must identify specific program components, audience groups, audience characteristics, utilization patterns, costs, or effectiveness in a way that can easily be analyzed by audience group, program element, manager, organization, or other specific dimensions. Averages are generally not specific. If the "average satisfaction" rating is low, for example, why is it low? Who rated it low? What groups rated it low? What elements created the low rating?

Specific detailed information typically requires granular data from your learning management system (or other enrollment and registration system). We discuss the importance of implementing consistent assessments and standards in your LMS later in this book.

2. Actionable Information Is Consistent. In order for information to be actionable, it must be consistent from program to program to enable comparisons across programs. For example, to measure learner satisfaction with an instructor, the same scale must be used for all programs to compare instructor against instructor. We found in our research that consistency is far more important than depth. Consistent "indicators" that apply to the programs can offer tremendous actionable information (see section, "How 'Indicators' Best Measure Training").

Note: Throughout this book the term "indicator" refers to some measurement (for example, satisfaction with the instructor, satisfaction with the classroom) that is captured directly from a learner or manager and tends to "indicate" impact, effectiveness, alignment, or other measures. A "measure," by contrast, is an actual business measure, such as sales volume, error rate, production rate, and so on. The reason we emphasize the use of indicators is that they can be captured in a consistent way from program to program. (In Chapter 6: Measurement of Business Impact, we discuss techniques for capturing and measuring real business outcomes.)

For example, an end-of-course assessment question that asks "How well, on a scale from 1 to 10, did this course help you improve your effectiveness at your current job?" is an indicator of utility. A question such as "How strongly would you recommend this course to others in your department (10 = strongly recommend, 1 = not at all)?" is an indicator of utility or alignment.

Neither of these questions actually captures business impact data directly, but they do capture consistent data, which, when captured across thousands of learners and hundreds of courses, will give you tremendously actionable information. Captured as indicators, such data will immediately show you courses that have "high utility" versus "low utility"—even though you have not tried to measure the actual utility itself. A course that scores low in utility would warrant an in-depth analysis of the program elements, audience, delivery techniques, and so on.

3. Actionable Information Is Credible. Finally, to make information actionable it must be believable. That is, you should avoid indirect correlations with business measures that are not 100 percent attributable to training.

Now this principle may be a bit controversial. Many books have been written describing techniques for linking learning to direct business results. While this exercise clearly has value, we have found that in most cases such efforts fall into the category of "projects," not "processes," and as you will read later, one of the keys to a successful measurement program is to focus on repeatable processes.

The information you capture must stand up to testing from non-training business people (people outside of the L&D function). If you compute the return on investment (ROI) of a sales training program, for example, and then claim some credit for a resulting sales increase, then be ready to defend that claim. The vice president of sales may feel that the sales increase cited is a result of a great sales team, while the vice president of marketing may believe it is a result of a great marketing program.

Averages May Not Deliver Actionable Information

Another important principle: use caution when employing averages. Average information (for instance, average satisfaction level, average scores) may not give actionable information and can be misleading.

Let us look at a contrived but very realistic example. Suppose the average learner satisfaction rating for one course is 3.7, and for another, it is 3.9 (see Figures 1.1 and 1.2, respectively). Presumably, this would indicate that the second course was of higher value.

Figure 1.1 Course 1. Satisfaction Average of 3.7

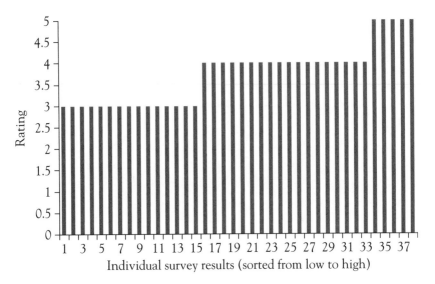

Individual survey results (sorted from low to high)

Figure 1.2 Course 2. Satisfaction Average of 3.9

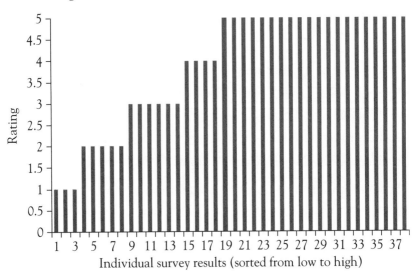

Individual survey results (sorted from low to high)

Figure 1.3 Comparing Detailed Satisfaction Scores

	Number of ratings	
Rating	Course 1	Course 2
5 (excellent)	5	20
4 (good)	18	4
3 (fair)	15	6
2 (poor)	0	5
1 (dismal)	0	3
Average satisfaction	3.7	3.9

Using the idea of actionable information, a training manager might then try to figure out what was "wrong" with the first course to identify areas where the first course could be made more like the second course.

Let us go beyond the averages and dive into the data. Figure 1.3 reviews the actual distribution of satisfaction levels shown in Figures 1.1 and 1.2. The actual data presents a completely different story.

For Course 1 (the lower-rated course), there were no "1" or "2" low ratings. Although only 13 percent of the learners were "thrilled" with the course, most found it to be "fair" to "good"; 58 percent rated the course "good" to "excellent." This course is a pretty well rated course.

For Course 2, (the higher-rated course *whose average rating rates it the* "best practice" course), 60 percent of the learners rated the course between "good" and "excellent," with half of the learners being "thrilled" and rating it a "5." Yet, 21 percent of the learners hated the course (rating it a "1" or "2") and 36 percent gave it a rating of "3" or below. This course had some problems.

Which course is really "better"? The average does not answer this question.

Looking at the detailed distribution of satisfaction ratings tells the real story. The first course is an average course; it more or less gets the job done, and seems to be reasonably well liked. The second course is probably a much better course but demands a more specialized audience. The data shows us that it had a number of the wrong people in attendance; hence, it was poorly "aligned." (We have an entire chapter on alignment in this book.) The detailed data we have obtained is now highly actionable.

If this was your course you would want to characterize the differences between the people who did not like the course and those who did. Perhaps the people who liked the course are the more senior managers? Perhaps the people who did not like the course were from a certain country? Many actionable findings could be captured from this information.

The purpose of this contrived example is to show why it is so important to "dive into the data" to obtain actionable information. As this example illustrates, detailed data—by audience, by session, by date, by platform—will give you insights you can act upon.

Again, the key to obtaining such detailed data is to create standard measurement indicators and capture them consistently across many programs and many learners.

2. A Measurement Program Should Not Be Designed to Cost-Justify Training

The second principle we would like to discuss is the trap of using measurement to cost-justify training investments or programs. Many times the biggest driver for a measurement program is a mandate from above: "We don't trust what you're doing, so we want you to measure the impact."

"I really need help coming up with a measurement
strategy for our leadership development program.
Our management continually asks us how much
value we are getting out of this investment."
—Chief Learning Officer, Healthcare Provider

My experience with many organizations has shown that when the focus on measurement to cost-justify training investments, the measurement program rarely results in a repeatable, actionable process. But clearly the problem exists: How do you make sure the organization understands the value of your training? How do you prove its impact?

Let me discuss a few important thoughts here. First, if your training organization is well aligned with the business (and has in place a business plan, the right set of governance processes, and communicates vigorously, which we discuss later), the organization will clearly see value. In fact, if you develop an operational plan for training (and only about half of organizations do this), publish this plan, and transparently communicate your progress against this plan, and regularly enlist feedback, your business constituents will have confidence.

Second, if you do not have the confidence of line management, no amount of measurement will help your case. One of the CLOs we interviewed told me how he manages this process. He regularly interviews line executives throughout his organization and asks them, "Do you believe that organization development will help us to attain our business goals?" If they say yes, then he knows they will appreciate the value of his programs. If they say no, then he knows that no amount of ROI analysis or other impact analysis will convince them. Bottom line: Do not design your measurement program to cost-justify training.

Third, consider how other operational groups in your organization measure themselves. Does the IT department try to cost-justify every IT project? Does the facilities department cost-justify every facilities investment? Trying to cost-justify training spending is just as hard and uncertain as trying to cost-justify other business support functions, such as marketing, finance, facilities, and IT. These business functions add value by supporting the revenue-generating, customer-serving, or product-development organizations in the company. While these functions do not directly generate revenue or manufacture products, their value must be measured through their indispensable support, alignment with strategic initiatives, high levels of customer service, and contribution to the overall business strategy.

Think about how your IT department measures itself. Does it measure the ROI of the company's email system? No, that is assumed. The IT department measures the system uptime, how much it costs to operate, how well the data is protected, and how easy it is to use. These operational metrics are very useful and actionable—they tell the IT department what it must do to continuously improve. Does the organization talk about eliminating the IT department? Rarely—only if the IT department is not providing high levels of customer service and support of strategic business initiatives.

Consider the marketing department. Like training, marketing is used to influence behavior, which ultimately results in sales. Although the influence, alignment, and cost-effectiveness of marketing can be measured, organizations cannot directly measure its direct contribution to the bottom line. Marketing, like training, is measured by its operational efficiency, alignment, and other indicators that drive business results. Marketing measures its return to the business by looking at *indicators*: leads generated, hits to the website, or inquiries from direct-mail campaigns. Training is very similar.

3. Measure Training as a Support Function

The third important principle in measurement is that training is a business support function. As a support function, training exists solely to improve the effectiveness and efficiency of what we call "line of business" or "revenue and customer" functions. Consider Figure 1.4.

In any business there are two types of organizational groups: those that directly build products, generate revenue, or support customers (called "line of business functions" above)—and those that support these customer and revenue-generating groups (the

Figure 1.4 Training as a Business Support Function

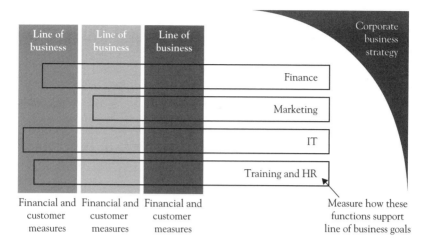

horizontal boxes). Sales, manufacturing, customer service, and other customer-delivery organizations fall into these line-of-business, customer facing groups. HR, IT, Finance, Facilities, and so on, all fall into the second category. These support groups exist in order to improve the performance of the true revenue and customer-facing operational groups.

What each type of organizational group should measure is different. Sales, customer service, and manufacturing should measure true business or customer output: dollars of revenue, number of cases closed, customer satisfaction, and number of units produced. Support groups, then, do not directly measure their direct impact on sales, customer satisfaction, and manufacturing quality—but rather how well they support these functions and their initiatives to drive outcomes. Although this may sound subtle, consider the following example.

Imagine that one of your business units (U.S. Sales, for example) tells you that their goals are to gain market share in the mid-market business segment by 30 percent through the launch of product A. Your goal in training is not to increase market share, but rather to support this group's goal of increasing market share. When you sit down with the executives of this group, you may find that they demand the following: new training to be delivered within 30 days of product launch, learner satisfaction of 4.5 or higher, a total training time of two days or less, a cost of $1000 or less per learner, and 90 percent adoption rating within 3 months.

Your goals and related measures, then, fully align with theirs. Your measures, as shown in Figure 1.5, are highly aligned, actionable, credible, and detailed. They fit our three criteria for actionable information. They are also very easy to capture.

If you sat down with the line business executives and established these criteria for success, you would find yourself very well aligned with their business goals.

Let's go back to the concept of an indicator. If you deliver a program that is delivered on time, on budget, with high satisfaction and utility indicators (more on this later), and excellent alignment with the business's known business initiatives, you will definitely see business impact. And the business leaders will be thrilled. If you also measure your internal efficiency and cost-effectiveness, you will be even more highly regarded.

**Figure 1.5 Alignment of Learning Objectives
with Business Objectives**

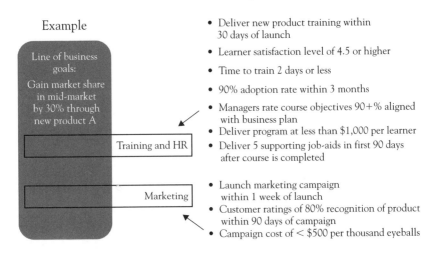

Example

Line of business goals:
Gain market share in mid-market by 30% through new product A

Training and HR

Marketing

- Deliver new product training within 30 days of launch
- Learner satisfaction level of 4.5 or higher
- Time to train 2 days or less
- 90% adoption rate within 3 months
- Managers rate course objectives 90+% aligned with business plan
- Deliver program at less than $1,000 per learner
- Deliver 5 supporting job-aids in first 90 days after course is completed
- Launch marketing campaign within 1 week of launch
- Customer ratings of 80% recognition of product within 90 days of campaign
- Campaign cost of < $500 per thousand eyeballs

Throughout our research we found highly effective training organizations that measured only a few things—but they were the things the business really cared about. They did not focus on trying to measure "level 2" or "level 3," except for highly exceptional, very expensive programs (such as leadership development) where the investment in evaluation is worth the effort.

Later in this book, we highlight many ways of using indicators to measure direct business impact (see Chapter 5: Implementation: The Seven-Step Training Measurement Process). In fact, our research finds that most well-aligned training organizations have dozens of measures of direct business impact.

Let us cite another example of how valuable these support indicators can be. One of the most successful retailers of home improvement supplies has developed a broadly deployed e-learning system that delivers courses to 120,000 employees through in-store kiosks. The courses delivered include programs on safety, loss prevention, new-hire training, and many types of product training (for example, lawnmowers, drills, saws, wood, and so on).

At the store level, the managers have a set of graphical, easy-to-read reports that display completion rates and total training compliance. This information is highly actionable at the store, regional, and divisional levels. This "exception reporting" tells managers which employees have not taken training or are behind on their training targets. Does it measure business impact? Not at all. Is it a key indicator of success? Absolutely.

The manager of this particular training organization periodically asks the retail managers about the value of the training. The answers he receives are invaluable: "We can get new hires up and running in only a few days." "Our training program is one of the most valuable tools we have for retention." It turns out that in retail (and many other industries) one of the biggest values of training is not sales productivity but retention. Training makes individuals feel more confident, which in turn increases their engagement and commitment to the company, which in turn increases their loyalty and productivity. Can this be measured directly? No. But can you obtain indicators of this success by talking to managers and looking at aggregate retention rates? Absolutely.

4. A Measurement Program Must Meet the Needs of Multiple Audiences

The fourth principle of training measurement is that you must consider the information needs of different audiences. Different audiences will expect and demand different levels of information.

The CLO and training leaders will be interested in efficiency, effectiveness, resource utilization, and on-time delivery. These measures should be developed in a way by which they can be benchmarked, and the measures should give specific detailed information that can be used to change and improve training operations.

The vice president of HR will be interested in training volumes, compliance, and spending per employee. These measures should be computed annually or quarterly, and compared against industry benchmarks.[2]

Line-of-business executives will be interested in how much training was consumed, which employees are and are not taking training courses, and how well the employees and managers feel their needs are being met. These executives are interested in measures such as scores, completion rates, satisfaction levels, alignment, and indicators of utility and impact.

First-line managers will want to see detailed results from their employees to help with development and performance planning. The managers want specific information on completion (exception reporting), utility, and learning results.

Trainers and instructional designers will want to see specific comments and feedback from learners on the quality and value of their particular programs. Comments and direct feedback must be captured and distributed on different program elements.

Each of these needs has value, and each requires a slightly different level of detail and way of presenting information. As you develop your measurement process, think about what is needed for each of these audiences, so that you capture information of value to the entire organization. By serving the needs of line managers and other executives, you have naturally created alignment. They will tell you what they need to know, which in turn helps you to improve your training organization to meet these objectives.

5. Measurement Should Be a Process, Not a Project

If you want an ongoing measurement program, you should not think about measurement as a series of "evaluation projects," but rather as an operational process that captures continuous, actionable information. There is a cost to measurement: it takes time, energy, and tools. Successful high-impact organizations focus on developing a simple, easy-to-implement, *repeatable process* that can be used over and over again. What our research has found is that less data, measured in a repeatable and consistent way, is far more valuable than a small number of highly complex, custom measurement projects. When you find extraordinary information (for example, a program that is failing miserably or a very expensive program that is not meeting expectations), then you can embark on one or two evaluation projects.

Consider Figure 1.6. If you let program managers try to measure the efficiency, satisfaction, and impact of their programs through individual, program-oriented evaluation projects, the workload would look like the triangle on the left. You will spend a lot of time and energy focusing on data capture, leaving little time and energy for analysis. You may be able to standardize

Figure 1.6 Measurement as a Project Versus Process

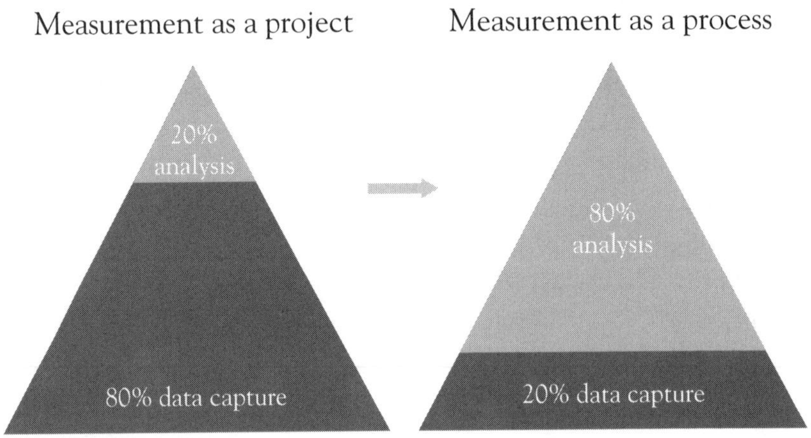

Measurement as a project   Measurement as a process

20%
analysis

80% data capture

80%
analysis

20% data capture

the evaluation process, but you will find that you do not have enough time or resources to cover all your training needs and likely will spend far too much time capturing information to really analyze it well.

On the other hand, if you implement a simple but repeatable process that crosses all of your programs, the workload will look like the triangle on the right. And if you use approaches like the ones in this book, the information you capture will be very detailed and will cover all elements of the program, from design through delivery and impact. By thinking "process" versus "project" then, you will find yourself asking "What can I measure that will apply to all our programs," rather than "What can I do to evaluate a single program." The result will be a highly efficient and actionable set of data that will help you decide when, if ever, you want to embark on an individual evaluation project of a single program.

In the quest of such a process, consider the value of measuring the same indicators across all training programs. If you did establish eight to twelve standard indicators for all learners and all managers in all programs, you would quickly start to see wide variations among programs, instructors, media, audiences, program types, and more. You would be able to compare the outputs and efficiency of programs against each other. You would be able to show line management and other managers how your programs are improving over time. And you would be able to quickly see "outliers"—programs that are highly effective or efficient when compared to others. You will learn more about how to do this when we discuss the Impact Measurement Framework®.

How do you establish standard measures? As Figure 1.7 shows, best-practice organizations typically develop three sets of standard indicators or surveys: first, the standard indicators for all learners in instructor-led training. These questions will typically include questions about the facility and instructor, in addition to impact questions from our framework. Second, they develop a set of standard questions for learners at the end of an e-learning or blended program. These differ slightly because of the delivery media. Third are a standard set of questions for managers, which reflect alignment, utility, and other impact measures. We will describe these three sets of questions later in this book, but for now it is important to understand the principle of thinking "process" not "project."

Figure 1.7 Standard Indicator Sets to Consider

Learner		Manager (Learner's Manager)
Instructor-led training	Standard indicator set 1 (8–12)	Standard indicator set 3 (8–12)
e-Learning or blended program	Standard indicator set 2 (8–12)	

Assign a Process Owner

An important step in creating this measurement process is to assign one person or one group to own the development, monitoring, and reporting of the process. Our High-Impact Learning

Organization[3] research found that organizations with a single person (or small team) who owns the measurement process are as much as 11 percent more efficient in their overall training operations. Each program manager cannot be asked to define his or her own way of measuring a program—measurement is a specialized process that takes focus. Each program manager should implement the process, but the process itself should be defined and monitored by a single person. This person can then train program managers in its implementation, analyze data across programs, and evaluate results.

This measurement person or team can focus on the following important questions:

- What are the goals of this measurement strategy? What decisions do we want the data to support?
- What operational plans do we have in our training organization that we should measure and monitor?
- What operational measures and plans exist in the business units we support that we can align our measurement toward?
- How can our measurement process be made consistent from program to program?
- How can we make it easy to scale, without increasing numbers of staff required as we roll it out through more and more programs?
- How can we make the process easy to administer and drive a high level of compliance with the survey or other tools used to capture data?
- How can the data be stored so that it is easy to recall in the future and compare against new data? What analytics or LMS system will be best for capturing and analyzing this data?
- How can we most easily report and analyze the data we capture?
- Make sure the measurement approaches are "repeatable processes" and not "projects."

Measurement Versus Evaluation

There is a difference between measurement and evaluation. "Measurement" (as discussed in this book) provides the information and data for analysis. This data can be used to monitor, analyze, and evaluate every step in the learning process.

"Evaluation" refers to a process used to judge or determine the relative value of a given learning program. ROI analysis, for example, is a form of evaluation (not a form of measurement).

This book is focused on helping you implement a measurement program—describing repeatable processes you can implement across any program. If you follow the steps in this book, you will find it easier to decide when, if ever, you embark on specific evaluation projects. It is important to consider any form of evaluation in the context of a "model"—that is, a repeatable approach that enables you to evaluate programs in a repeatable, consistent, and credible way. The Impact Measurement Framework® described in this book presents such a model, which will help you with the evaluation of individual programs. That said, we will use the term "measurement" throughout this book to discuss the processes and measures that capture actionable, specific, and credible information.

6. The LMS Is a Foundation for Measurement

Learning management systems play a very important role in a measurement program.

Consider the vast and important actionable information in your LMS. The LMS has all the source data for learners themselves, their roles, languages, locations, and managers; employee enrollments, completions, times in courses, certifications, and scores; course descriptions by category, type, vendor, and modality; and many other important dimensions such as competencies, career plans, and even performance ratings. These elements are the actionable "dimensions" in your learning measurement program.

In addition, almost all LMS systems have an online assessment tool that can be used for end-of-course surveys. These tools always have the most basic question types you need for end-of-course surveys. Most also have built-in analytics tools, which could be used to analyze and format information for a variety of audiences.

Most organizations are not tremendously satisfied with their learning management systems. In fact, our 2007 research found that 24 percent of LMS owners are considering or planning on switching LMS systems. Despite the challenges of selecting and implementing these systems, it is important to realize that one of the biggest business benefits of an LMS is its ability to capture, analyze, and deliver information. In fact, when we ask organizations that have had an LMS for two years or more to describe the biggest benefits they have seen, measurement and data are ranked number one.

For those companies without an LMS, this should not stop the measurement process. Many organizations scan or type end-of-course surveys into spreadsheet applications and other tools, to gain the value of a consistent and repeatable measurement process.

Need for Data Standards in the LMS

Since the LMS is considered the "single source of truth" for assessments, completions, and other information, you will find it critically important to create data standards. For example, comparing several courses with inconsistent names against each other may prove difficult or impossible (for instance, which of the two hundred courses in "safety" should be compared against each other?). With e-learning, if some courses have Aviation Industry CBT Committee (AICC) and Sharable Content Object Reference Model (SCORM) tracking and others do not, it will not be possible to compare completion rates or other volumes across courses. Once the elements to measure have been determined, establish some data standards, so that all the data collected in the LMS is consistent and complete.

Standards should specify how courses are named, how they are grouped, what assessments are used for e-learning courses versus ILT versus self-study, and how learners are grouped. Without such standards, analysis of the large volumes of LMS data you will receive is difficult. This book will help managers understand the types of standards that are necessary.

7. Dedicate Resources

In our High-Impact Learning Organization research,[4] eleven different organizational elements of corporate training were reviewed to identify what structure, initiatives, and programs drive the highest levels of effectiveness or efficiency. One organizational decision that has a major impact on results is the creation of a dedicated measurement team (or person). Organizations with some dedicated measurement resource are 11 percent more effective and 9 percent more efficient than those without.

Why is this? Simply because the measurement of training is complex and takes focus. Additionally, since we highly recommend that your measurement program be consistent across all programs, someone must develop it, steward it, train others in the steps you use, and run reports and analyses. This person or group can also evaluate the many models and techniques for data capture and evaluation, and they can develop and refine the ongoing measurement process.

Large, well-run training organizations typically have a measurement person or group: At Sprint University, an organization with more than three hundred employees, there are several people responsible for measurement. At AT&T Wireless, with a national training organization of more than 150 people, three training staff members are dedicated to measurement. United Airlines has two dedicated measurement staff members. The

IRS has an entire evaluation and measurement team dedicated to measurement.

Even if you are a small organization, at a minimum, there should be an employee who "owns" the measurement process on behalf of the entire organization. This employee develops the process, trains program managers in its implementation, works with the technology team to implement tools, and analyzes program results and other data. In general, the total measurement effort should only cost 2 to 4 percent of the total training budget.

8. Start Simply and Evolve Over Time

The final principal to remember is that training measurement takes patience. There are so many possible things to measure. Our research reveals that organizations with successful measurement programs start simply and grow over time. Initially, training volumes, standard Level 1 satisfaction surveys, and standard measures of client satisfaction may be a good start. Developing these measures into a consistent and repeatable process is a huge achievement.

Over time, you should create a set of standard end-of-course surveys and implement a process to measure alignment. Start measuring costs and metrics against your plan, and implement a standard process for business impact. Every organization we studied grows its sophistication and maturity over a period of years. Rather than trying to measure everything from the beginning, establish a simple but process-based approach, and then gradually add more information and target greater audiences over time.

Notes

1. An operational business plan for learning is typically built to support the general business plans for products, revenue, services, and other primary business functions. As a support unit,

the training plan should establish annual goals and objectives that support each strategic goal or initiative. Typically, these plans include strategy, budget, program plans, organizational model, operational measures (number of courses, enrollment objectives, etc.), alignment with HR-talent management initiatives, major capital investments (i.e., a new LMS), and major commitments by quarter. Such a business plan should be widely circulated and signed off by all major business units. It "commits" the L&D function to deliver against this plan and forms the basis for operational measures.

2. For more information, see *The Corporate Learning Factbook: Benchmarks for Learning Organizations*. Bersin & Associates/ Karen O'Leonard, May 2006. Available at www.bersin.com.

3. For more information, see The High-Impact Learning Organization: WhatWorks® in *The Management, Organization, and Governance of Corporate Training*. Bersin & Associates, June 2005. Available at www.bersin.com.

4. Ibid.

Chapter Two

The Pros and Cons of Using ROI

Much has been written about the importance of measuring the ROI (return on investment) of training programs. ROI is frequently positioned as the "ultimate measure" of training effectiveness. In fact ASTD[1] "ranks" organizations on their effectiveness by whether or not they use ROI measures. While ROI has its benefits, we are not big fans of focusing on this approach. This chapter discusses the pros and cons of using ROI.

First, it is important to realize that ROI measurements are not used as frequently as one may think. When we interviewed High-Impact Learning Organizations,[2] we consistently heard resistance to using ROI as a core focus of their measurement programs. Rather, these organizations focus much more heavily on operational measures and use ROI occasionally for a few very special projects. This research showed that only 10 percent of organizations even attempt to measure business impact and fewer than 5 percent regularly measure ROI.[3] Figure 2.1 shows routinely tracked information.

Why this low level of usage? Our research found that measurement of ROI is time-consuming, often inaccurate, usually not very actionable, and rarely credible. While the concepts of ROI are important and can be used for specific high-value projects as part of the performance consulting process, I believe you should use ROI sparingly. At the end of this chapter I will explain some very high-value, easy ways to use the ROI concepts.

Let me now discuss a number of pros and cons of using ROI.

Figure 2.1 Information Routinely Tracked

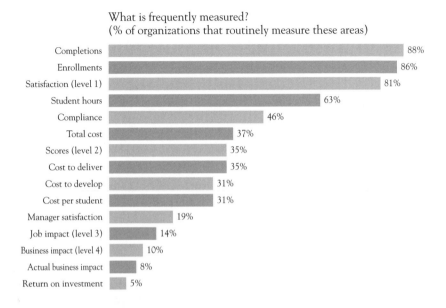

What is frequently measured?
(% of organizations that routinely measure these areas)

Completions	88%
Enrollments	86%
Satisfaction (level 1)	81%
Student hours	63%
Compliance	46%
Total cost	37%
Scores (level 2)	35%
Cost to deliver	35%
Cost to develop	31%
Cost per student	31%
Manager satisfaction	19%
Job impact (level 3)	14%
Business impact (level 4)	10%
Actual business impact	8%
Return on investment	5%

ROI Analysis Assumes That Training Is Treated as an Investment

First, let us discuss the basic principles of ROI measurement. ROI analysis is not something new. The concepts have been around for years and were designed (as taught in business schools) to measure the financial return over time from a fixed capital investment, such as a machine or building. The word "return" refers to some financial income that is captured over a period of years, and the term "investment" refers to a capital investment (not an expense). ROI analysis was designed to help a company *prioritize capital investments* and solve the problem of asset allocation. It has very specific meaning to a business or finance person.

It was designed to answer questions such as:

- Should we invest in Machine A to improve productivity or continue to do things manually?

- Is Machine A (a very expensive machine) a better investment than Machine B (a less expensive, but perhaps less robust model)?
- Should we spend money on a new manufacturing process or on hiring more salespeople? Which is a better long-term investment?
- Should we buy a new company or build out a product ourselves?

Suppose a profitable company makes $100 million of profit each year. One of the big decisions to make is where to invest the $100 million to optimize the company's growth and profitability. To answer this question, companies look at a list of possible investments and rank them based on their ROI.

ROI analysis also has the concept of a "hurdle rate." The "hurdle rate" is a company's existing cost of obtaining new capital (the cost of issuing debt or raising money in the public markets). To a financial analyst, a winning investment must generate a return (ROI) that is greater than the company's existing return on other investments (the company's so-called "hurdle rate"). For example, if the company is currently generating a 15 percent return on assets, it would clearly be a mistake to invest in a new project that generates a 5 percent return on assets (unless the company felt this investment was necessary to offset some other risk).

The key to ROI analysis (from a financial perspective), then, is that:

- Investments are made over a period of time, so the return may take many years to realize (and the investment itself may take place over a period of years);
- Investments should be compared against each other to help prioritize them;

- Investments should always generate a return that is greater than some established "minimum"; and
- ROI analysis should be done before the investment is made so that the exercise helps decide whether or not to invest.

Now, let us consider whether training programs fit into this model. Is the training budget considered an investment that delivers return over time? Are you willing to compare the ROI of training programs with the ROI of other investments in the company? Do you have a "minimum ROI" for which you are ready to compare your programs? Typically, the answer to all these questions is no.

Unfortunately, in almost every company I talk with, training costs are considered an expense (similar to all of HR and IT). The funds spent on training are charged against income in the current year, so there is no way to "allocate" this expense to a multiyear payoff. And even though we all know that training generates returns over many years, in most companies it is necessary to re-justify or re-budget training dollars each year.

Let me cite an example. One of our research clients (an electric utility) performed an extensive ROI analysis of an operational training program. He computed an ROI of over 2,000 percent (more than a 20 times return per dollar invested). He then made the mistake of presenting this finding to one of the finance executives in the company.

This executive looked at the result and became quite agitated. He said to the training manager, "Do you know the return on investment we generate across the entire business of generating electricity? It is around 5.5 percent. What your analysis is telling us is that we should shut down our power plants and get out of the business of generating electricity and focus exclusively on training. Am I to believe this?"

This is why we discourage organizations from an overfocus on computing the ROI of training—it is not the correct financial model. The simple version of ROI taught by Jack Phillips (benefits − costs)/(costs) is really a computation of potential cost recovery, and should probably be called something else. When you throw around the term "ROI," business people hear the words "return" and "investment" and think very different things than what you are truly computing.

So how should you analyze your financial impact on the company? Going back to the issue of training being a support function, remember and accept the fact that training is a cost center. Your job in managing a cost center is to develop a well-aligned operational budget that conforms to corporate guidelines and benchmarks.[4] You should compare yourself to others in your industry and make sure you are spending the right amount of money in the right places. Of course you should try to measure the business impact of your programs, but do not build analyses that assume that training itself is generating revenue or profit. If every support function in the company did this type of analysis, we would see the "ROI" of IT, the "ROI" of management, the "ROI" of buildings and grounds, the "ROI" of the security guards, the "ROI" of the phone system, and on and on. When you added these all up, you would see that every dollar of revenue is probably being captured 20 to 30X by these different support groups.

How do you justify your expenses and ask for more money? Remember that any expense dollars allocated to training are coming out of some other expense budget in the company (they do not come out of incremental revenue). Your goal in managing this budget is not to compare and optimize this spending against other long-term investments (such as plant and equipment); but rather to *prioritize these programs within the budget and make sure the company is receiving the highest possible impact at the lowest cost from each. You should justify your investments through benchmarking and industry-wide comparisons.* You should try not to use it as a way to "cost-justify" or "grow" your budget.

There are excellent ways to use the ROI concept, and these are discussed later in this chapter.

In-Depth ROI Measurements Are Often Difficult to Believe

One of the risks of using ROI analysis is that you may run into someone who attended business school who rigorously questions your analysis. As the electric utility example describes, exposing ROI measurements may put you at the risk of losing credibility. Consider the following challenges that are likely to trip you up:

1. Can You Really Compute the True Cost of Training?

The only way ROI makes sense is if you know what the "I" is—the total cost. The total cost of training is much more than the cost of development. It is the cost of:

- Development and all the "burden" of development tools and systems;
- Materials and consumables used in delivery;
- Instructor preparation and delivery time, burdened with the instructor's salary, benefits, and other costs;
- Delivery expenses through technology, such as the "burdened" cost of your LMS, amortized over years;
- Students' salaries for the time spent in training and travel expenses; and
- The opportunity cost[5] of the students' attendance (the lost opportunity of these people not doing their real jobs during the time of training).

If you glibly leave some of these out, a financial analyst may want you to go back and compute them all. Very few training organizations have a cost-analysis system set up to capture these costs.

2. Can You Isolate the Effects and Compute Their Return?

Of course this is the biggest challenge. Time and energy must be expended to identify a quantifiable measure that can be considered a real financial return (for example, a sales increase). Even after computing such a measure (and making all the assumptions necessary), it is very hard to correlate this directly to training. If you believe you increased sales, the VP of sales may argue that in fact the sales increase was for another reason (e.g., the fantastic performance of his team, the attractiveness of a new product, marketing programs, etc.).

3. If You Compute ROI, Can You Determine Whether a Computed ROI Is Appropriately High?

Suppose you do compute an ROI. How do you determine whether the ROI is high enough? Is 100 percent ROI good or bad? What are you comparing it against? Suppose the vice president of sales noticed that the training department got an ROI of 200 percent on a certain program that cost $500,000 to develop and deliver. And suppose that "return" is an increase in sales revenue. Seeing this return might cause the vice president of sales to claim that a much higher return would have been achieved by *hiring two additional sales representatives*, with each representative generating five to ten times his or her salary in sales, for a 500 to 1,000 percent "return." Your ROI number may feel good but, when compared with the many possible investments throughout the company, it may fall far short. Are you prepared to compare your ROI on training against other true investments in the company? Can you be sure that the ROI you compute, if it is believable, is really the best use of the company's funds?

In Concept, the ROI of Training Should Be Extraordinarily High

This takes us to the next point. What *is* a reasonable ROI for training? When I read examples of companies that generate a 67 percent ROI or 125 percent ROI, I wonder: Should we even consider these as "high" or "low"?

Conceptually I believe well-developed training creates a very high ROI—ten to one hundred times the investment (hence thousands of percent ROI). It should be, since training is one of the most far-reaching and highly leveraged expenditures in your organization. Let me explain why.

Consider the following numbers: Training investments are typically only 2 to 3 percent of payroll; yet, they improve the productivity and effectiveness of that other 97 percent to 98 percent of payroll spending. If these investments are not generating ten to one hundred times their return, then I would question whether this money could not be better spent elsewhere. Although measurement of this return is difficult, the whole premise of training is that it is a highly leveraged resource across many employees who are consuming and spending many, many dollars. Executives who understand the value of employee development know this, so they invest year after year—even without scientific ROI analysis.

Consider the sample numbers illustrated in Figure 2.2: The Financial Leverage of Training. Training typically consumes 2 to 3 percent of payroll, and most companies' revenues are five to fifteen times their payrolls. This means that training expenditures as a percent of total sales are very small (from two-tenths of a percent to half a percent).

This small expenditure is designed to improve the effectiveness and efficiency of this tremendously large number—the revenue and profitability of the entire company. If a training program increases sales by a few percentage points, for example,

Figure 2.2 The Financial Leverage of Training

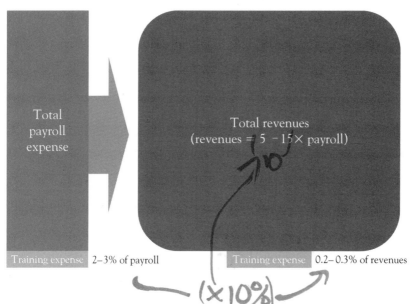

Training expense 2–3% of payroll   Training expense 0.2–0.3% of revenues

the leverage is huge. Suppose, for example, that half of the entire training budget was allocated to sales training. If this budget (which would correspond to, say, two-tenths of a percent of sales) increased sales by only 1 percent, the ROI of this expenditure would be 500 percent. We believe this is a highly conservative assumption. Therefore, any training program that does not truly generate 500 to 1,000 percent ROI (measured on sales) is falling short of its potential!

Figure 2.3 shows such numbers for a company with $100,000 in sales.

As this simple and conservative example shows, a very small investment in sales training (in this case, half of the entire training budget) can have a huge impact on revenue or profitability. The argument here is not that training does not generate an ROI but, rather, that the ROI, although difficult to measure, should be very high—far higher than most organizations can compute through ROI projects.

Figure 2.3 Conservative ROI in Training

The financial leverage of training expenditures

Total company sales	$	100,000	
Payroll	$	15,000	15%
Training expenditures	$	375	2.5%
Training as % of sales		0.38%	

$$100k / 375 =$$

Return on investment of sales training as an example

1. 1/2 of training spent on sales training	$	187.5	
2. Training increases sales by 1%	$	1,000.0	1%
3. Return on this spending		533%	

$$1 + \frac{(1000 - 187.5)}{187.5} =$$

It Is Very Difficult to Correlate
Outcomes Specifically to Training

We all know this. While many books and techniques can be used to try to correlate outcomes to training, in almost every case I have seen these correlations are easy to argue with. Here is an example.

When I was involved in the development of e-learning programs for Circuit City, it was decided to try to measure the ROI of a particular program—an e-learning program focused on training store salespeople to sell extended warranties (a highly profitable product). The training was deployed to a select number of stores. Then sales of extended warranties in those stores were measured and compared to the sales of the same product line at stores that had not participated in the training. The test period lasted approximately sixty days (that is, sales results were examined for sixty days following the training program).

The results were analyzed by salesperson. A chart was developed that compared sales of extended warranties for the salespeople who took the training to the sales of those who did not. The results showed that those who took the training sold approximately 3 percent more in revenue than those who did not. This seemed good enough; then this result was multiplied by the total number of stores operated by Circuit City. The determination was made that this particular program would generate millions of dollars in revenue and profit for the company.

However, the impact of other factors was ignored. At the request of Circuit City, a statistician was hired to further analyze the data. The statistician looked at many variables, including the age of the salespeople, their length of employment with the company, their job levels and other demographics. The statistician found that, while the "average" of the trained sample did sell more products, the *cause of this sales improvement was not the training.* By correlating many factors into the sales improvement, the statistician, in fact, determined that the training itself was only responsible for less than half a percent of the improvement in sales.

The factor that had the highest correlation (or greatest cause) for sales improvement was "time with the company." It turned out that salespeople with more experience with Circuit City were selling 200 to 300 percent more extended warranties than new salespeople. Since the sample of trained sales representatives just happened to be slightly biased toward experienced employees (a complete accident), the "trained population" had just enough increased seniority to show a 3 percent higher increase in sales.

So we have to assume that "isolating the effects of training" are difficult and often suspect. Before you embark on a serious ROI project, think about the "ROI of ROI analysis"—Will the project itself generate enough return to justify the time and energy to capture the data? Can you easily and credibly compute the "return"?

(Despite these challenges, there definitely are ways to directly capture business impact data from training. I discuss several ways of directly correlating training to business impact in Chapter 6: Measurement of Business Impact.)

How Do You Make ROI Actionable?

The final challenge with the use of ROI is that ROI analysis, when conducted as a project to evaluate a single program, is rarely actionable. Measuring the ROI of a single training program does not tell you how well it may compare against others in your portfolio. It rarely tells you which elements had the most or least impact. And it does not usually bear up to comparison against other investments in the company.

On the other hand, some companies have found ways to use the ROI concept to make it more actionable—by essentially computing "potential ROI" before developing a program. Let us now discuss this approach.

Use of "Potential ROI" During Performance Consulting

So where does ROI fit? One of the most valuable uses of ROI is to use the concept during the needs analysis or performance consulting phase. In other words, compute ROI *before* you even start developing a program.

How do you do this? Keep it simple. Using the signoff form from your business manager (we will discuss this in detail later) and your internal performance consulting process, identify the size of the problem to be solved (in dollars), the potential savings you believe you can achieve (being reasonable), and the planned program budget. You can then compute a "prospective ROI" easily. The key here is to be very reasonable about the potential performance improvements and to gain buy-in from the business owners in developing this number.

For example, suppose your vice president of sales asks you to develop a sales and technical training program for a new product line. You determine that the total sales goal for this product for the next year is $30 million. Working with your VP of sales, you agree that this sales program is likely to have a 3 to 5 percent impact on sales productivity overall. The program, then, has a potential benefit of 4 percent of $30 million, or $1.2 million. If the program costs $500,000 to build, the potential ROI is:

$$\frac{(\text{Benefit} - \text{Cost})}{\text{Cost}}$$

$$\frac{(1.2 - .5)}{.5} = 1.4 \text{ or } 140 \text{ percent.}$$

Now this number may or may not seem high relative to other investments in the company, but when used at this phase you see two things: first, it is positive, illustrating that it may in fact be worth spending $500,000 on this particular program. Second, you can now look at the 140 percent potential ROI and compare it with other possible programs and investments. For example:

Are there other sales enablement programs that may generate a higher ROI? What if we spent less on this product rollout and spent more on the overall sales training career curriculum?

Is 140 percent too low when compared to all the other programs you are building? Perhaps the $500,000 budget is too high and we need to find a way to increase the "potential ROI" up to 300 percent or more by cutting the cost and possible benefit? (Notice that the biggest increases in ROI come when costs of the program are cut, not when benefits are increased.)

Generally such "potential ROI" analysis is very valuable at this phase, because it aids in the needs analysis process as well. Consider the other benefits of regularly using this simple process:

- It forces the program manager to clearly investigate the root causes of a problem and how these can be solved.

- It illustrates the potential benefits to the business managers who are sponsoring the training program.
- It helps the organization decide what level of investment is appropriate for this particular program.
- It helps the organization prioritize this particular program against other programs.

Both HP and Caterpillar use this simple process. An excellent way to implement this is by adding such calculations into the "signoff form," forcing both the line of business manager and the training program manager to work together to both compute the potential benefits and scope the potential budget.

If you institute this process, you will naturally want to compute the "actual ROI" at the end of the program. Here my suggestion is to keep it very simple or use approaches like the "Success Case Method," developed by Dr. Robert Brinkerhoff. Brinkerhoff's five-step approach uses examples and case studies to identify actionable information about the real benefits of a given program.[6]

"Performance-Driven" Versus "Talent-Driven" Training

The use of ROI is not going to go away. Despite its many limitations, it is a conceptually simple approach to understanding how different programs compare in their value. Ultimately, however, in order to use ROI concepts well you have to consider one important factor: the nature of the problem you are solving.

Let me digress here and discuss an important point. Broadly speaking, training programs fall into two categories: performance-driven programs and talent-driven programs.

Performance-driven programs are those programs designed to solve specific performance problems. For example, if you determine that managers in your company are inadvertently creating sexual harassment claims, you would purchase or build a one-or-two-hour sexual harassment training program. This program would be designed to solve this problem. Similarly, if you find that your call center representatives are entering the wrong information into your online service system in certain fields, you would develop a one-or-two-hour program designed to teach them how to use the system correctly and avoid these problems.

Many of your training programs are designed for these types of problems. These programs are typically fairly easy to build, fairly easy to deliver, and it is relatively easy to compute a potential ROI (you measure the change in the actual performance problem). (See Figure 2.4.)

Figure 2.4 Performance-Driven Versus Talent-Driven Learning Programs

	Performance-Driven Learning	Talent-Driven Learning
Drivers	Business performance issues in operational units and functions	Talent and leadership gaps, critical skills shortages, engagement and culture
Goal	Develop individual capabilities and fill performance gaps	Develop organizational capabilities driven by competencies, not performance
Examples	Sales training, customer service training, field service certification	Multi-tier leadership development new-hire onboarding programs
Organization	Aligned by job within function	Aligned to all job roles in job function
Timeline	Months or even shorter	Multiple quarters to years
Complexity	Functional	Enterprise or divisional-wide
Integrated with	Product launches, new service offerings, geographic expansion	Performance management, recruiting, succession planning
Challenges	Performance consulting, program design, manager engagement	Resource allocation, program design, job alignment, manager adoption
How to measure success	Solving business problems: sales, service, quality, turnaround	Filling and solving talent gaps (ie., shortages, recruiting goals)

The second type of learning program we build are what I call "talent-driven" learning programs. These programs develop rich and complex skills and deliver in-depth levels of information that solve many problems. In fact, they "develop people" rather than "train people." In the example of sexual harassment, you may find that, in fact, managers not only have problems in this area, but they also have problems in coaching employees, evaluating employees, communicating, conducting meetings, and goal setting. In fact, you may find that what you need is an entire management curriculum (leadership development or management training program) to address these problems.

This second approach would involve development of a much longer, richer development program that may include instructor-led training, online training, special assignments, assessments, and more. The cost of developing and delivering this rich, longer-term program are likely to be 10X the cost of building the performance-driven learning solution. And the rollout time and complexity will be much higher. Such programs include onboarding, leadership development, and other forms of long-term career development.

How do you measure the benefits of such talent-driven programs?

For talent-driven learning programs, computing ROI will rarely be meaningful. These programs are designed to solve many problems and generate many benefits. They typically have broad and large benefits such as.

- Improvements in employee engagement and satisfaction
- Improvements in retention
- Improvements in the ability to hire
- Improvements in work quality
- Improvements in cycle time through increased communication and teamwork

As I discussed earlier, these benefits will generate very high ROI, but are difficult or impossible to measure. So what should you do?

Rather than embark on a long-term one-or-two-year ROI analysis, we suggest you take a different approach. In our research and discussion with clients, we found that the programs with the highest ROI are the programs that are best aligned with the most urgent and important problems of the business. Alignment is one of the most important measures we discuss in this book (see Chapter 7: Measurement of Alignment). If you align the program well, developing a strong agreement on its value, goals, and target audience, the impact will be large. You can then use the other techniques in this book, along with the Success Case Method by Dr. Brinkerhoff, to identify specific examples of how this program is driving value.

Going back to the Circuit City example cited earlier, we found that after all the ROI analysis was complete and many years of e-learning had been delivered, one of the biggest impacts from product and sales process training was developing *confidence* in the retail sales force. This confidence led to retention, engagement, and a commitment to work hard and contribute to the company. In a large organization like Circuit City, a 1 percent increase in retention is worth tens of millions of dollars per year. While it took us many years to realize and gain perspective on this return, ultimately it showed us that these talent-driven training programs were of high value and freed us to work on capturing more specific, actionable information.

Don't Let ROI Become "Return on Insecurity"

One of the traps training managers fall into is using ROI to cost-justify a large or questionable program. A training director in our research made the comment that he considers ROI to be "return on insecurity." His premise is that ROI analysis is an attempt by training managers to try to justify their existence. His argument is that, when training programs and processes are well aligned with urgent business needs and a well-defined performance consulting process is in place, the training professional will never be asked to compute ROI.

I have generally found this to be true. Spending your time building a solid performance consulting and business alignment process is far more valuable than implementing ROI projects on existing programs.

We recently discussed the topic of training measurement with the CLO at Saks Fifth Avenue. Saks has a very well-developed enterprise learning program, which includes in-depth training for managers, buyers, and retail salespeople. They have an advanced e-learning solution built on a proprietary platform, which delivers training to every Saks store in the country. Saks' "Business of Buying" program is considered one of the most strategic investments the company has made.

When we asked the CLO whether she was asked to measure the return on all these investments, she told us "never." Their programs are so well aligned with the needs of the business that no one at Saks has questioned the value of this ongoing investment in learning.

Notes

1. ASTD: American Society of Training and Development, the U.S. industry trade association for corporate training.
2. For more information, The High-Impact Learning Organization: WhatWorks® in *The Management, Organization, and Governance of Corporate Training*, Bersin & Associates, June 2005. Available at www.bersin.com.
3. This survey data was captured during the summer of 2006 from 136 large organizations (demographics are available in Appendix III). Interestingly, this survey was also conducted in 2004 and the results of the two surveys are almost identical.

4. For more information, see *The Corporate Learning Factbook®
   2007: Statistics, Benchmarks and Analysis of the U.S. Corporate
   Training Market*, Bersin & Associates/Karen O'Leonard,
   February 2007. Available at www.bersin.com.
5. "Opportunity cost" is defined as the actual "lost opportunity"
   from students attending training instead of doing their regular jobs. It is usually computed by totaling up the employees'
   salaries—but in reality the costs are higher. They include the
   cost of travel, time away from work, and the loss of productivity (sales, production, and so on) that is not taking place during training.
6. Dr. Robert Brinkerhoff. *The Success Case Method: Find Out
   What Is Working and What Is Not*. San Francisco, CA: Berrett-
   Koehler, 2003.

Chapter Three

Limitations of the Kirkpatrick Model

In discussions with many training managers and executives, I found that one of the biggest challenges organizations face is the limitations of the existing measurement models (primarily the Kirkpatrick model). If you were a sales manager and were asked to measure your sales organization, you would focus on measuring sales revenue. Then, as you became more sophisticated, you would start to measure revenue per salesperson, revenue per customer, time to close a sale, number of leads per month, and many other things. There is a "causal" model behind sales: more leads lead to more opportunities, more opportunities lead to more deals, and more marketing increases the number of leads. These measures are easy to understand, easy to measure, and highly actionable.

In the case of corporate learning, however, we are faced with a more daunting task. Today (before this book) we do not have such a causal model. The only widely understood models for training measurement are the four-level Kirkpatrick model and the Phillips ROI Methodology™ (a methodology that has been popularized by Jack Phillips focused on techniques to compute and use ROI).

My research has found that these models, while easy to understand, have limitations. While almost every training manager knows what the Kirkpatrick model is, few organizations can "fully implement" it. The reason for this is that the model is incomplete and somewhat out-of-date. As I tried to develop a set of best practices and tools to help our research clients,

I found that first it was necessary to "move beyond" much of the thinking in the Kirkpatrick model. While the model has value as a thinking tool, our research has found that in order to implement a sustainable measurement program you must extend your thinking beyond it.

The Kirkpatrick model divides training measurement into four basic levels and Jack Phillips adds ROI as a fifth (Kirkpatrick does not consider ROI the fifth level, but for the purposes of simplification, we will include it in this list). The Kirkpatrick model establishes the following levels:

- *Level 1: Satisfaction (Reaction)*. Did the learners like the program? What was their reaction?
- *Level 2: Learning*. Did the learners learn what was intended?
- *Level 3: Application or Job Impact (Behavior)*. How well did the training impact on-the-job performance? Did behavior change as a result of this training?
- *Level 4: Business Impact (Results)*. How well did the training impact business performance? Did the business see results?
- *Return on Investment: ROI (Phillips)*. What was the financial return on investment (ROI) from the program?

These five "levels" are widely recognized and used by training managers all over the world. They benefit from simplicity: they are easy to understand. They use words and concepts that are clear to training managers. However, our research has identified limitations in the Kirkpatrick approach that make training measurement difficult. Let me explain why.

The Kirkpatrick Levels Are Not a Complete Model

First, although it is easy to understand, the Kirkpatrick model is not really a complete model: it does not attempt to explain how training drives learning or how training drives impact. It simply points out that it would be nice to measure these four things. There is no set of steps or application concepts that make the levels useful.

Let me clarify. In the case of the sales measurement model I briefly described above, it is clear that "leads" create "opportunities" and "opportunities" create "sales." If you believe in this "causal model," then sales operations are easy to understand and measure: first you measure leads, then you measure the number of opportunities developed from these leads, and then you measure the sales driven by these opportunities. Together, this simple three-level model gives you tremendous insights and actionable measures. If you have a track record of one opportunity for each one hundred leads, and you launch a new marketing program that generates two opportunities for each one hundred leads, then you know you have done something exceptional that should be repeated. If, by contrast, you launch a campaign that generates only one opportunity for every two hundred leads, then you know you are under-performing. This model, and its underlying measurements, are easy to understand, related, and actionable.

In the case of the Kirkpatrick levels, no such model is given. The four levels are not causally related at all. Consider the levels themselves. Satisfaction or reaction does not necessarily lead to learning, and learning does not lead to behavior or job impact. And it is not true that job impact or behavior always leads to business results. In essence then, the four "levels" are simply four interesting things to measure. They are not directly related to each other.

In addition, the four "levels" are not parallel in language or construction, making them even more confusing. Considering the principles we discussed earlier, let us look at what the four levels really are:

"Satisfaction or Reaction" is a measure in itself, which can actually be measured on a numeric scale. One can easily measure satisfaction with a simple survey or interview.

"**Learning**" is a term that connotes a highly complex concept: the concept of gaining knowledge, skills, and abilities. It can be measured through assessments, but in reality, as we all know, it must be measured through on-the-job observation and behaviors. One can pass a test without truly "learning" very much. And in the business world, application-based learning is far more valuable than book learning. It connotes the concepts of deep levels of skills, ability, judgment, and certain behaviors. It is far more complex and different than satisfaction, which is a fairly simple thing to measure.

If we wanted to measure learning in a parallel way to satisfaction, we should rename this level to "scores" or "percent of mastery score" (the AICC definition). This would be more parallel to satisfaction.

"**Behavior or Job Impact**" is an even more vague and unclear term. It describes an outcome that is neither a measure nor achievement of a task. This term can be interpreted in many ways (for example, increasing efficiency, increasing quality, increasing production volume, and so on). "Efficiency," "quality," and "volume" are terms that are parallel to "satisfaction"; yet, these types of terms are not used in the model and are left to the implementer to consider.

It is obvious to any training manager that "job impact" is a major goal of training. The Kirkpatrick model points out this fact, but gives us no information on how job impact is created, what factors lead to job impact, or how one would actually measure it. Hence most training managers stop at Level 2 and spend many hours (and often thousands of dollars) trying to "measure Level 3."

Again, if we go back to our sales model, we know that "sales revenue" is the goal, and that leads and opportunities are the drivers of this sales revenue.

"**Results or Business Impact**" is the most difficult measure of all and can be interpreted in hundreds of ways (for example, increasing sales, increasing profits, increasing market share, improving retention, and so on). The concept is clear and obvious, but again, the Kirkpatrick model does not tell us how satisfaction, learning, or job impact lead to business impact. Can we assume that Level 3 leads to Level 4? Or are they independent?

We all know that the business impact of training is driven by many complex factors, including culture, business alignment, management buy-in, marketing, and other factors (which we discuss in our model). The Kirkpatrick model piques our interest, but again gives us no real help in measuring this important goal.

"ROI," as discussed earlier, actually has a specific definition. ROI is the financial return on a capital investment measured over a period of time. It requires measurement of business impact over time and computation of costs over time, both very difficult to measure reliably and even harder to measure consistently across every training program.

Witness the effect of this confusion by looking at what training organizations actually do measure. As Figure 3.1 shows, whereas satisfaction (Level 1) is measured 81 percent of the

Figure 3.1 What Is Routinely Measured (Bersin Research)

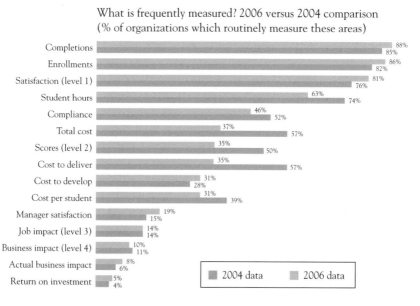

What is frequently measured? 2006 versus 2004 comparison
(% of organizations which routinely measure these areas)

	2004 data	2006 data
Completions	85%	88%
Enrollments	82%	86%
Satisfaction (level 1)	76%	81%
Student hours	63%	74%
Compliance	46%	52%
Total cost	37%	57%
Scores (level 2)	35%	50%
Cost to deliver	35%	57%
Cost to develop	31%	28%
Cost per student	31%	39%
Manager satisfaction	19%	15%
Job impact (level 3)	14%	14%
Business impact (level 4)	10%	11%
Actual business impact	8%	6%
Return on investment	5%	4%

time, business impact and job impact are measured far less frequently—and the anecdotal evidence reveals that even these numbers are far overstated. Most studies show that fewer than 5 percent of programs actually measure business and job impact in a consistent and actionable way.

The most disappointing part of this data is the trend. From 2004 to 2006, most indicators show flat or a reduction in the amount of measurement taking place. To reiterate, this is not because the model is hard to understand but, rather, it lacks specificity and gives the user inconsistent terms to think about, which leads to the second limitation with the model.

The Model Incorrectly Positions the Levels as a Hierarchy

One of the problems in the Kirkpatrick model is the concept that the four levels are a causal hierarchy. Given my comments earlier that the "levels" are inconsistent in their specificity and language, they are made even more difficult by leading practitioners to believe that they should strive to "move up the hierarchy."

Consider Level 1: satisfaction (reaction). Level 1 surveys are often called "smile sheets" to denigrate their importance. Organizations I talk with are often embarrassed to promote a sound Level 1 measurement program, because so many practitioners ask "That's nice . . . but how do you measure Level 3? Isn't that what we're *really* supposed to measure?"

Again and again, practitioners are led to believe that they should start at Level 1 and "move up the pyramid" to Levels 2, 3, and 4. ASTD and other organizations rank and score companies by the percent of programs for which they measure Level 3 or 4, or ROI, implying that it is somehow "better" to measure those levels. A general assumption exists that it is "better" to measure ROI than it is to measure learner satisfaction.

I disagree. Remember that our goal is to capture actionable information. Learner satisfaction is one of the most important measures we have. If used well, learner satisfaction measures form the basis for many of the indicators we use to measure impact and alignment. Consider some of the subtle and powerful ways learner satisfaction can be captured: You could ask, "How well did this course apply to your specific job requirements?" or "How strongly would you recommend this course to your peers?" While these sound like "satisfaction" questions, they are actually far more powerful. They measure job impact, alignment, and utility—all actionable measures that vary widely from program to program. The Kirkpatrick model would group them all into the category of "Level 1." While the other levels have value, I believe most organizations can benefit tremendously from a much better implementation of "reaction" measures.

The Kirkpatrick Model Ignores the Role of Training as a Service-Delivery Function

The third limitation in the Kirkpatrick model is that it ignores the important role that corporate training plays as a service-delivery function. As we discussed in Chapter 1, in the business world, training is a means to an end: the function exists only in the context of its value to the sales, manufacturing, service, and other operational business areas.

The Kirkpatrick measurement model only considers measurement of training "programs" themselves. It does not cover the processes of business alignment, performance consulting, operational efficiency, time-to-market, and customer satisfaction, which are critical to success as a training organization.

Our High Impact Learning Organization® research has shown how corporate training has evolved from the Corporate University (1980s and 1990s) to Learning Shared Services (late 1990s to today) and now to a new model reflecting the increasingly important role of corporate training as a talent management function.

In the Corporate University structure,[1] corporate training function is run as an organization (like a university) with a collection of training "programs." The organization purchases and develops these programs, markets them, and delivers them to a broad audience. In this organization employees "come to the university" to be trained and programs are assembled into curricula and offerings.

In today's business and technology environment, training organizations are far more complex than universities. They are not simply a collection of programs; rather, these training organizations are internal *service delivery organizations*, which serve as performance consultants, technology managers, content development organizations, and delivery teams. Their focus is on responsiveness to business needs and strategic talent management initiatives. The Kirkpatrick approach was developed during a time when the training organization was a team of almost all "trainers." Today, the delivery function is less than 60 percent of most training organizations' head count[2]—and frequently far less—illustrating how training organizations have evolved.

As a result, the four-level Kirkpatrick model misses important service-oriented measures that training managers must monitor. These include important measures such as training volumes (yes, "butts in seats" is a very significant measure), training efficiency (as a service function, development and delivery efficiency is an important measure of excellence), program alignment (the single biggest issue that plagues program managers), audience compliance, program utility, alignment with business strategies, delivery on-time and delivery on-budget.

Let us consider an example. Suppose a vociferous call center manager in the organization demands a training program for new managers that focuses on critical, new quality procedures in the call center (such as the process of verifying customer credit).

This program is considered business-critical so a complete blended-learning approach is developed that includes pre-work, online modules, a classroom module, and an end-of-course exam.

Unfortunately, due to the complexity of the design, the program takes ninety days longer to build than expected. But this is what the business needs.

The course is launched. Employees start enrolling; good satisfaction ratings (Level 1) are received and exam scores are high (Level 2). To try to measure Level 3, a few managers are asked how they liked the course; these managers politely respond that it seems to fill the gap.

But the call center executives are upset. The course took three months longer to build than was expected and was way over budget. The course's modular approach is confusing the call center reps—many of whom skipped the online modules and waited for the instructor-led program before studying. In addition, the long duration of the program means that managers have to wait many months before seeing any significant impact.

Since this program may not be well-regarded, an ROI analysis is performed. A group of employees who completed the course are studied and the results are compared with employees who did not take the course. The employees who completed the training are much more accurate at verifying credit, so the ROI of this course is computed to be very high. Yet, there is a lot of grumbling among the call center management team, and it is very hard to get people to enroll and complete the program.

What happened?

Using the Kirkpatrick model of measurement, the training succeeded. For a corporate university, the course would be considered a success; but in the real world (the business world), this program is less than successful. Some of the problems include:

- **Inadequate Needs Analysis.** The time-critical nature of the problem was not truly understood and the program was over-engineered;
- **Insufficient Audience Analysis.** It was not understood that this particular audience would not accept any online learning;

- **Lack of Business Alignment.** The business managers wanted this program done urgently, and development on-time was a business-critical need; a major criterion for success was missed; and

- **Poor Prioritization.** Too much time and energy were put into this program; a simple half-day or two-hour instructor-led training (ILT) course may have fixed the problem along with, perhaps, an online performance support intervention or job aid as a follow-up.

A sound measurement model should measure all of these important processes. Using the Kirkpatrick model alone, these important factors in a program's success would not be monitored or measured.

This simple example gives a sense of why we need to go beyond the Kirkpatrick model. As helpful as it is, it is limiting. Companies must move beyond Level 1 and Level 2 to a more business-centric measurement framework.

Kirkpatrick Misses Other Operational Measures

Finally, the Kirkpatrick model misses other important and actionable measures that managers must consider. Look back at the items routinely measured in Figure 2.1; many of these are not even mentioned in the model.

A few of these measures (which we include in the Impact Framework®) include:

- Was the program delivered on-time and on-budget?

- Was the target audience attracted to the program? What percent of the target audience attended? Why or why not?

- Is the program the right length? Did it meet the company's needs for time away from the job? Could or should it have been shorter (or longer)?

- How efficient was the program to develop and deliver? How much did it cost compared to other similar programs? Did the company get its "money's worth" when compared with other programs? (This is similar to ROI, but is more process-focused.)

- How well-aligned was this program to the strategic portfolio of problems in the organization? Did this program, perhaps, crowd out other more important programs? How well do the line-of-business managers and executives buy in to this program?

- Did the audience have the correct motivation and support to complete the program? One of the biggest factors in success is how well the audience itself is motivated to learn. Did their managers give them the time off from work? Will their workgroup support their learning when they return to work?

- Did the learners have the right skills before they came to the program? Perhaps they were overqualified or under-qualified?

- If the program was a customer or channel program, how much revenue or customer satisfaction did the program generate? Is it meeting its revenue targets and, if not, why not?

- What are the long-range retention rate and impact of this program? How long-lasting is its impact on our organization? Does it reinforce or hurt the company's culture?

- How accurate and precise is the content itself? How well was the business problem identified? Did collaboration with subject-matter experts (SMEs) ensure the program delivered information, skills, and competencies that are correct and useful?

- How is this program benchmarked against similar programs? Did the organization overspend or under-spend on this program?

These are important business measures that should be considered by any learning organization.

One Alternative: The Six Sigma Approach to Measurement

One example of a business-oriented measurement approach that illustrates the need to go beyond the Kirkpatrick model is the Six Sigma approach.

Remembering that training is just another business process (such as sales, accounting, or manufacturing), the process can be measured by comparing it with other such processes. The training director, Depository Trust Clearing Corporation (DTCC), one of the highest volume transactional businesses on the U.S. stock exchange, applies the Six Sigma approach to training.

In the Six Sigma methodology (widely adopted in manufacturing and other business processes), success measures are defined by the customer, not the service department. The term "Voice of the Customer" is used to describe these success measures. In one program developed by DTCC, the requirements are shown in Figure 3.2.

DTCC Learning uses this approach to identify its clients' needs before the department starts developing any programs; these needs then form the basis of its evaluation process. In some cases, these measures are easy to obtain. (See Chapter 5, Step 2: Establish a Performance Consulting Process).

Another Alternative: The Success Case Method™

Another approach that focuses on program evaluation is the Success Case Method™ (SCM) developed by Dr. Robert Brinkerhoff. This methodology uses surveys and interviews to identify trainees who have been highly successful recipients of a given program. It then analyzes the causes and magnitude of their

Figure 3.2 DTCC Learning Sample Six Sigma Measures

Voice of the customer	Key customer issue(s)	Critical customer requirements
What does the customer want from us?	We need to identify the issue(s) that prevent us from satisfying our customers.	We should summarize key issues, and translate them into specific and measurable requirements.
Customer doesn't want to install additional software.	Develop course with software that requires plug-ins.	User experiences are seamless.
The course runs without crashes or hangs.	Pages takes more than 20 seconds to load.	Pages take no more than 30 seconds to load.
Screen layout is clear.	Not adhering to design standards.	Adhering to design standards.
Pre– and post–test.	No test.	Courses have quizzes, pre– and post–test.
Be able to enroll using online assistance.	No tutorial.	Enrollment tutorial is available and learner successfully enrolls without additional assistance.
The program (course) should be 2½–3 hours.	Poor classroom management techniques.	Ensure practice and learn meets time and constraints.

successes to help the program manager understand what really works (and what does not work). This approach is a very practical, useful alternative to ROI. It gives you an easy-to-follow, powerful recipe for surveying and interviewing learners and identifying actionable information for program improvement.

I find this approach very practical and useful and I recommend that readers consider SCM as one of your tools for program evaluation. While it does not attempt to build a complete end-to-end measurement model, it is a very useful and powerful tool for program evaluation.

Notes

1. For more information, see *The New Learning Landscape: Death of the Corporate University*. Bersin & Associates, March 2006. Available at www.bersin.com.

2. For more information, see *The Corporate Learning Factbook®* *2007: Statistics, Benchmarks and Analysis of the U.S. Corporate Training Market*. Bersin & Associates/Karen O'Leonard, February 2007; and The High-Impact Learning Organization: WhatWorks® in *The Management, Organization, and Governance of Corporate Training*. Bersin & Associates, June 2005. Available at www.bersin.com.

Chapter Four

The Impact Measurement Framework®

Now let us move into solutions.

After dozens of interviews with learning and development managers and a review of many different approaches to measurement, I cataloged hundreds of measures and techniques. Many of these were widely "outside" of the Kirkpatrick model. To make these findings easy to understand and use, we developed a more modern and complete model for training measurement we call the Impact Measurement Framework®.

The goal of this framework is to give training managers and executives a complete and updated model from which to build their measurement programs. It is not a recipe, but rather a series of well-researched measures and approaches you can immediately use. No organization will adopt the entire framework in year 1, but over time you will see that each element of the framework adds new actionable information.

Let me also describe how this framework was developed. Rather than just collecting various measures to capture, we spent some time thinking about the entire end-to-end process that training organizations use to add business value. In other words, we tried to build a "causal model." Just as in the sales measurement example described in Chapter 1 (where "leads" lead to "opportunities" and "opportunities" create "sales"), we need a causal model in training from which to derive relevant measures. If we believe in this causal model, then we can select the measures at each stage to understand how and why a program is or is not working. The result: highly actionable information.

I named this end-to-end process the Business Impact Model®, and the Measurement Framework® derives from this model. You should be able to apply the framework to any step in the process you want to understand. Because the framework matches the Impact Model at each step, you can use the two together to build a "cookbook" for developing a measurement program.

What value is the framework? First, I hope it will educate you and help you understand each of the elements of training that drives value. Second, it will give you many easy-to-implement ideas for measures and approaches that can be implemented quickly. Finally, as you embark on your measurement journey, the framework (Figure 4.1) can serve as a roadmap to help you advance and improve your measurement program over time.

Let us now begin with the Impact Model®.

Figure 4.1 Using the Impact Measurement Framework

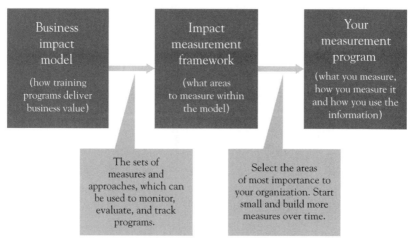

The Business Impact Model®

As I talked with many companies about their challenges in measuring training, I realized that, in order to measure their effectiveness and efficiency, one had to make many assumptions about how training programs actually work. If you want to measure the soundness of your car, for example, you have to understand that oil temperature and water level are important indicators of engine health. In the same way, if we want to operationalize the measurement of training, we need to know what elements of training really matter—which elements drive impact.

The model is titled "Business Impact" for a reason: it attempts to decompose all the elements of a training program that drive business impact. Remember that, unlike traditional education, in corporate training every single outcome is a means to an end: improving business performance.

As shown in Figure 4.2: The Business Impact Model, there are three major parts of this model:

Figure 4.2 The Business Impact Model

Four phases to business impact

1 Problem definition	2 Training solution	3 Individual performance improvement	4 Organizational performance improvement

Training processes

Business alignment	
Performance consulting	Measurement and feedback
Program development and delivery	

Elements which influence impact
(programmatic, environmental, and organizational)

		Existing skills/knowledge
	Program design	Learner motivation
Problem identification	Targeting and marketing	Learner attitude
Root cause analysis	Learning experience	Manager support

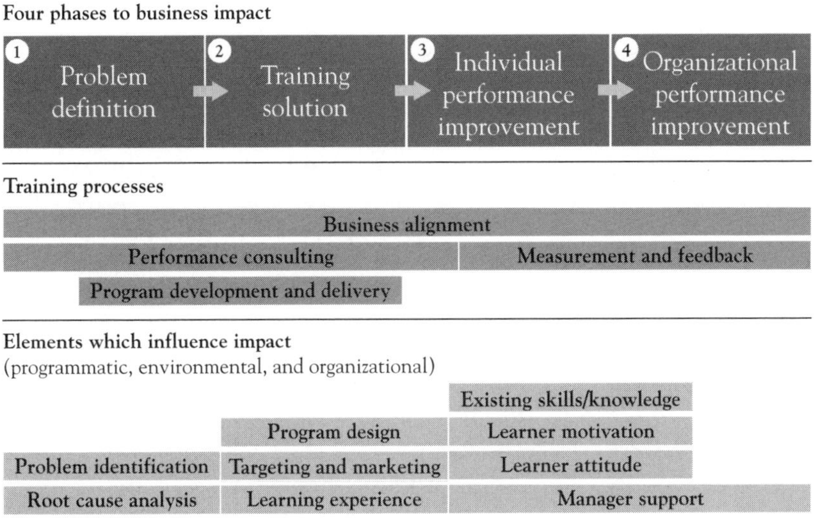

1. The four *phases* of a training solution (depicted horizontally at the top);

2. The specific *training processes* that support each of the four phases (shown in the middle); and

3. The *program, environmental, and organizational elements* that thereby influence business impact (depicted at the bottom).

The model is designed to be simple, easy to understand, and consistent across the four phases. This is how it works.

How the Business Impact Model Works

Each business impact phase is supported by a training process (that is, something the training department does), and a set of processes and environmental issues, which drive results. If you agree that this model makes sense, you can measure one of the processes or elements to capture actionable information about your training programs.

Let us step through the four training *phases*:

1. Problem-Definition Phase. The first phase of a training solution is the most important—the challenge of clearly defining the problem to be solved. As any training manager knows, often the problem presented is very vague: "We are not selling enough product A so we need some training" or "Our manufacturing process is creating errors and we need training to improve quality" or "Our new employees need onboarding."

This process includes identifying, quantifying, and defining the business problem, making sure that this problem is aligned or well-prioritized by the business, and understanding its causes.

The first process in problem definition is a critically important phase I call "business alignment." In this phase you work with the business managers and your executive team to make sure you have prioritized, diagnosed, and scoped the problem to be solved. In this critical phase you understand that a problem exists, you interact with the line manager to scope its size and priority, and you gather requirements about the type of solution the line manager desires. (One of the critical ways to measure business alignment is through a manager check-off form, which we discuss in Chapter 5: Implementation: The Seven-Step Training Measurement Process.)

The second process in problem definition is "performance consulting" (also called "needs analysis"). Performance consulting (a well-documented process) is the process of unraveling the business problem to its root causes, identifying the learning components of these causes, and developing a set of learning and informational plans to solve the problem. The output of performance consulting is a very clear set of learning requirements and a clear understanding of how the root cause of the problem will be solved through this learning.

Let us use an example to explain these two critical processes. Imagine that your company suffers from lackluster sales of a new product. First, the training manager must make sure this is a well-recognized problem that the vice president of sales feels warrants the time, money, and effort to solve through training (business alignment). During this step, the training manager should quantify the amount of sales the vice president feels is being "lost." They should gain approval to consider training as a solution and make sure that the managers are willing to let salespeople spend the time in training to solve the problem. Sign-off forms and interviews are a good tool to use here.

The second step (performance consulting) is to now research, study, and understand the root cause of this problem which, in turn, will lead to a set of learning objectives. For example, through a series of interviews and field meetings, the training manager may find that one root cause of low sales of the new products is the sales representatives' inability to understand and explain the value of the features under certain well-known customer objections. This is clearly a learning problem that can be addressed by a training solution. This phase is one of the most important steps in design and measurement.

The measurement of these two processes, business alignment and performance consulting, is very important. If you aren't solving the right problems, it doesn't matter how well the programs work. One of the CLOs we interviewed told me that her single most important measure was asking her training directors to give her the prioritized list of the business problems they were addressing in their respective business areas. She then matches this list against the list of business priorities she receives from the business managers themselves. This gives her a powerful "dashboard" for alignment.

2. Training Solution Phase. The second phase in training is development of the training solution itself (where you probably spend much of your time). This phase includes the process of designing, building, targeting, launching, and delivering the training program itself. Using the information obtained through the business alignment and performance consulting process, the training organization now builds the appropriate training program and schedules and performs its delivery. The business impact from this phase is influenced by three key elements.

A. Program Design. Most training managers believe that this is where the core value resides. While design is clearly a critical element, other elements can also make or break a program. Factors that influence design include:[1]

- The learning objectives;
- Specific skills to be imparted;
- Audience characteristics, such as size of audience, language, existing skills, age, time to learn, experience, seniority with the organization, access and familiarity with technology, and many more;

- Budget for the program itself;
- Location and availability of technology;
- Skills available in the learning organization;
- Time available to build the program and time available for delivery;
- Other programs that complement, supplement, or compete with this program.

B. Targeting and Marketing. In addition to program design, the second area in the development and deployment phase is the process of targeting and marketing:

- How well was the right audience defined and targeted?
- Do we have the right people in attendance or taking the course?
- How clear are the objectives to learners and their managers?
- How well were the learning objectives matched to the audience? Did we clearly understand the background of these people? Was the course made relevant to their needs and work environment?
- How well could the learners identify the right program? Was it clear to them that this was the course to take?

Although these issues seem less important, they can become critical if not handled well. Many of these issues revolve around the role of first-line managers:

- Do managers know the right people to enroll in the course?
- Do these managers support the course's value and the time commitment required?
- Do managers understand the schedule, pre-requisite, and time requirements of the program?

C. Delivered Learning Experience. And the third issue in program design and delivery is the delivered learning experience. Here there are many factors involved:

- How effective was the instructor at delivering the material?
- How well did the technology work?
- How comfortable was the learning environment?
- Did the experience itself help or hurt the learning and business outcome?

The learning experience is dependent on many things: instructor capabilities, quality of materials, quality of e-learning experience, seamless delivery of technology, effective use of audio/video and simulations, quality of collaborative experience, ability to interact with instructors and subject-matter experts, pace, and so on. Learning experience is a very popular area to measure because it often best reflects the learners' direct satisfaction. Such satisfaction may not be quantifiable or scientific, but it is always relevant to the business effectiveness of a program.

We know, for example, that training programs that are "fun" and "memorable" do leave a long-lasting impact. On the other hand, for some programs (for example, leadership training) the instructor's personality, focus, and experience are more important.

In an e-learning program, the learning experience includes such things as speed and ease of use, quality of graphics, sound, and video, and ease of interactivity through the mouse or other input devices. These delivery issues vary widely from event to event.

3. Individual Performance Improvement Phase. The third phase of business impact is what happens to the learners after they go back to their jobs. How well did the individual learner grasp and apply the material to improve his or her performance? How well did the learning actually apply? What tools or job aids did they bring back that they can apply? How does the program itself support the learners over time, as they continue to improve their performance?

Ultimately, performance improvement is our goal—but rarely do training managers consider how to make this "transfer" phase successful. Ultimately, if you want to measure this phase of the program, we believe there are four environmental and organizational issues:

A. Existing Skills and Knowledge. What was the existing level of knowledge in the learner? Specifically here we should ask questions such as:

- What level of background did the learners already have, and was the program too introductory or too advanced?
- How well did the learners already understand the material to be presented and was the program consistent with their existing knowledge?
- Where did the program fit into their already existing level of experience in this area?

If a learner's existing skills and experience are in conflict with the program, no amount of design or learning experience will drive impact. Typical ways to measure existing skills and knowledge are through pre-program assessments. Most advanced e-learning systems (LMS and LCMS systems) and courseware also allows the program to skip introductory material based on this pre-assessment.

Notice that this topic is not considered a "satisfaction" or "learning" issue, because it really relates to how well the program drives performance improvement. If the program is not correctly positioned based on the learner's existing knowledge, the learner's performance improvement will be small.

B. Learner Motivation. Learner motivation, the second performance improvement factor, is one of the most important influences on impact.

- Does the learner care about the program? Has it been positioned in a way that makes the learner want to learn?
- How motivated is he or she to learn? Was he or she given the right level of support, compensation, time, and management approval to take the program?
- If the program is mandatory, does the learner really care about the program, or is he or she just taking it to receive a completion certificate?
- Are the learners in this program the type of employees who want to learn and improve?
- How well did the manager give incentives and coach the learners to attend and receive value from the program?

Many factors influence motivation, and it should always be considered as part of the design and knowledge transfer process. One of our clients, Yum! Brands, embarked on an organization-wide learner survey to ask their employees how well prepared and motivated they were for available training programs. This research provided the organization very valuable information on the need to further inform and motivate managers to prepare employees for training.

C. Learner Attitude. Learner attitude is directly related to motivation.

Attitude, of course, is a highly subjective measure. The issue here is "readiness to learn." Did the learners come to the course with an open mind? Did they have enough time to leave their work environments and actually engage in the training process? How can training managers make sure that learners really want to learn this material and stay engaged during the learning process? Typically, attitude is driven through program design, alignment with line managers, and a design that appeals to the particular learners to be addressed. Simple questions such as, "How well did this course engage you in the learning material" and "How receptive were your employees to this course (asked of managers)" can gauge attitude.

D. Manager Support. How well does the manager support this program?

Much of our research continues to show that first-line managers can make or break an employee's development experience. Our High Impact Talent Management® research[2] found that the single management process that drives highest business impact is coaching: how managers coach and support their employees. A key part of such coaching is to help employees to understand how to build and execute their own development plans.

Such support directly impacts training results. If managers do not understand and support the information and skills being taught, the learners may find that the course was "interesting" (that is, satisfying), but difficult to apply on the job. The manager may even feel resentful that the individuals were away from work.

An excellent example of the power of manager alignment is a learning program we evaluated for a large consulting firm in Canada. This firm had been sending its consultants to a rigorous project management certification program that received very high marks in satisfaction and learning (Levels 1 and 2). The CLO felt proud of the program and its results and frequently promoted it to the organization.

She found, however, that when she later surveyed consultants on their ability to apply the program, results were poor. Consultants were not given time to use the processes they had learned, and management was not supporting the project management process through employee evaluation and project evaluation. In short, line management was not brought in.

In this case, the CLO operated a centralized country-wide training team that was somewhat disconnected from the day-to-day operations of the consulting groups. Once she identified the lack of alignment with line management, she set out on a mission to create a better education and governance process to make sure that line management was intimately involved in setting priorities, reviewing content, and supporting the project management program. Again, a business unit signoff process would have been highly beneficial here.

4. Organizational Performance Improvement. The fourth phase of business impact is more subtle yet. In this phase, hopefully, individuals take the skills, knowledge, and judgment gained by the individuals in the course and transfer this value to the overall organization. This fourth stage is typically described as Kirkpatrick's Level 4. While training programs focus on the skills and abilities of individual employees or customers, ultimately the benefit must be organizational.

What creates organizational impact? The two key factors here are alignment and management support. How well does this program align with other reinforcing values, programs, and processes in the company? Is it consistent with other management processes and measures? Does it use language and support processes that are well-known and widely used in the company? If it is inconsistent with values and management processes, it will fail at this stage.

Second, does this training program support and enhance a well-established management-driven business process? We hope it does. If so, not only will it improve the performance of the individuals, but it will also improve the operations of that process. If not, it may be an interesting and valuable course, but it will not be reinforced through organizational impact. The key here is for the training organization to build programs that are fully aligned with organizational business and known development strategies.

An excellent example of this situation is the management development program developed for a major accounting firm. The CLO was a highly motivated, creative training executive who developed a wide range of professional education and support programs to make sure that accountants at all levels had access to the latest laws and practices in corporate accounting. He developed a series of "learning channels" that include webcasts, conference calls, formal training, and group events that delivered a wide range of topical training conducted by both trainers and senior partners (Figure 4.3).

As the organization grew in the last few years, however, one of the bigger problems he identified was the tremendous need to hire new accountants and develop these people into future leaders of the company. The company was suffering from a lack of a

Figure 4.3 Accounting Firm's Learning Strategy

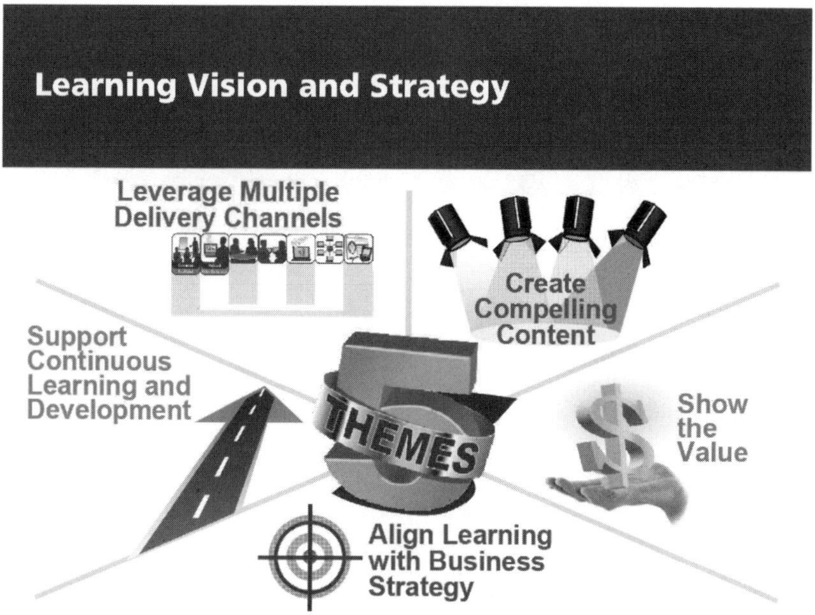

leadership pipeline, one of the biggest talent challenges facing corporations today.

By closely aligning with the business leaders of the firm, the CLO revamped the training curriculum into a series of programs (courses, events, development activities) they call the LEADS program, that integrates this curricula and a variety of programs into a complete career development program (Figure 4.4).

This program is clearly a "talent-driven learning program," as opposed to a "performance-driven learning program." It is focused on an organizational-wide talent challenge, not a specific business performance problem.

Performance Improvements for Talent-Driven Learning Programs. As we discussed earlier, there are two types of program: "performance-driven" versus "talent-driven." The former are traditional classes and courses that focus on solving a particular

Figure 4.4 Accounting Firm's Talent-Driven
Learning Programs

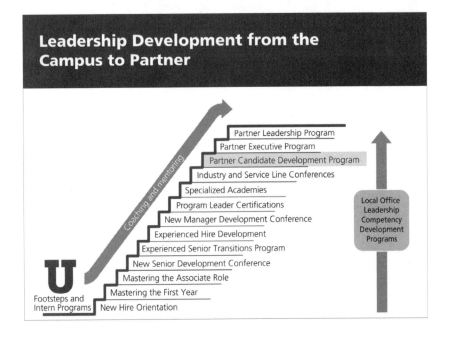

performance problem. These programs may include new product rollouts, customer service training, quality improvement programs, systems application training, technical training, and others. They are often driven through a performance consulting process and are designed to develop specific skills, knowledge, and capabilities to solve particular problems.

These programs are relatively fast to develop (months), relatively inexpensive to develop (tens to hundreds of thousands of dollars), and result in outcomes that can often be measured easily. For example, of you identify a problem with errors in the customer service process, you can develop a training program on customer service procedures that addresses these issues. You can then measure the "individual performance improvement" by looking at the reduction in errors and the "organizational performance improvement" by looking at the overall error reduction and improvement in customer satisfaction among customers who interact with the group that was trained.

On the other hand, talent-driven learning programs are very different. (See Figure 4.5.) These programs, like the one shown above, or a strategic leadership development program, or a long-term onboarding and career development program, focus on building talent. They do not focus on solving any particular performance problems, but rather on building organizational capabilities—developing better leaders, developing a larger pool of engineers, and so on. Ultimately, their benefits are measured in very different ways.

In the example of the accounting firm the benefits of their program are improvements in the leadership pipeline: more capable and confident managers ready to be promoted to partners. It also produces a better talent acquisition pipeline: new graduates look at the LEADS program as an incentive to come to work at the company it helps recruiters sell the company to high-powered accounting graduates.

These types of organizational benefits are far different from the typical "dollar savings" or "error reductions" we find in

Figure 4.5 Performance-Driven Versus Talent-Driven Learning Programs

	Performance-Driven Learning	Talent-Driven Learning
Drivers	Business performance issues in operational units and functions	Talent and leadership gaps, critical skills shortages, engagement and culture
Goal	Develop individual capabilities and fill performance gaps	Develop organizational capabilities driven by competencies, not performance
Examples	Sales training, customer service training, field service certification	Multi-tier leadership development New-hire onboarding programs
Organization	Aligned by job within function	Aligned to all job roles in job function
Timeline	Months or even shorter	Multiple quarters to years
Complexity	Functional	Enterprise- or division-wide
Integrated with	Product launches, new service offerings, geographic expansion	Performance management, recruiting, succession planning
Challenges	Performance consulting, program design, manager engagement	Resource allocation, program design, job alignment, manager adoption
How to measure success	Solving business problems: sales, service, quality, turnaround	Filling and solving talent gaps (ie., shortages, recruiting goals)

performance-driven learning programs. They tend to drive very large and different organizational benefits: improvements in retention, reduction in time to hire, improvements in employee engagement, improvements in the number of leadership candidates available for promotion, and improvement in job satisfaction. These are all areas that can be measured (the Gallup Q12 measures are good examples of surveys that measure these types of indicators), but cannot be measured through ROI or other Kirkpatrick approaches. In fact, in most cases, the organizational benefits of these programs are obvious.

So if you are working on measuring the fourth phase of our model, the "organizational improvement" phase, you should think hard about whether the programs you are measuring are performance-driven or talent-driven programs. If they are the former, you can easily find measures already being captured that will help you evaluate effectiveness. If they are the former, you are more likely going to want to talk with your senior VP of HR, head of recruiting, or other executives to look at the impact and effectiveness of these programs.

The Impact Measurement Framework®

Now, having discussed the various elements in each of the four phases of training, let us turn directly to measurement. As Figure 4.6 shows, there are nine measurement areas in the bottom section of the framework that allow you to measure and monitor each of these processes in corporate training.

Let us now examine each of the nine measurement areas, or "measures."

1. Satisfaction (Known as Kirkpatrick Level 1, or "Reaction"). Satisfaction is the granddaddy of all learning measures. We show it in phase two of the model, corresponding to the evaluation of program design, learning experience, and targeting and marketing.

As we discussed earlier, the word "satisfaction" has a specific meaning: it captures the learners' direct feedback on various aspects of the training program. But outside of this concept, it is a very broad measure. We can measure satisfaction with many things: program materials, instructor, specific exercises, alignment with business problems, and more. In fact, the Kirkpatrick model greatly diminishes the value of the broad range of satisfaction measures. I am a huge fan of satisfaction questions, if asked correctly. We use them frequently in our research. We will

Figure 4.6 Bersin & Associates' Impact Measurement Framework

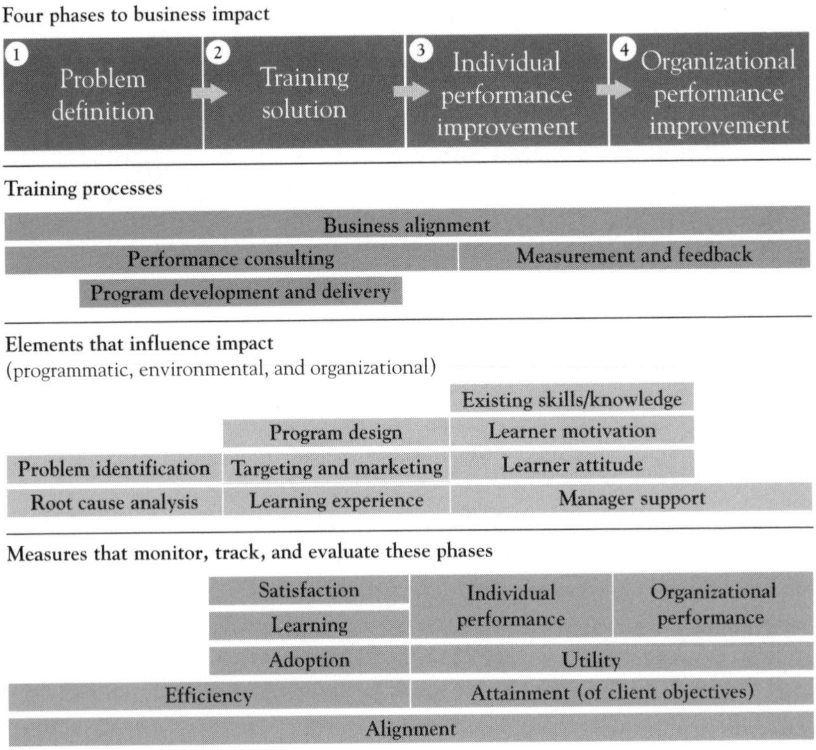

Four phases to business impact

① Problem definition	② Training solution	③ Individual performance improvement	④ Organizational performance improvement

Training processes

Business alignment	
Performance consulting	Measurement and feedback
Program development and delivery	

Elements that influence impact
(programmatic, environmental, and organizational)

		Existing skills/knowledge
	Program design	Learner motivation
Problem identification	Targeting and marketing	Learner attitude
Root cause analysis	Learning experience	Manager support

Measures that monitor, track, and evaluate these phases

Satisfaction	Individual performance	Organizational performance
Learning		
Adoption	Utility	
Efficiency	Attainment (of client objectives)	
Alignment		

describe how to use these measures in the implementation part of this book.

2. *Learning (Known as Kirkpatrick Level 2).* Why do we embark on training except to teach? All instructional designers and instructors would like to know whether the learning objectives of a training program have been reached. Learning outcomes (that is, scores or demonstrated abilities from training) help training managers understand how well the program design worked, how well the learning experience worked, and whether the right audience participated in the course. While learning does not tell us anything about business impact, it clearly measures how well the program achieved its training objectives.

The key to measuring learning, of course, is to try to figure out what "learning" you are trying to achieve. And measuring this "learning" is far more difficult than one may imagine. For example, if your training program includes a technical curriculum (like LSI Logic's storage training program for technical salespeople), the learning objectives may look like those in Figure 4.7.

These are clearly very complex learning objectives. They can really only be measured through on-the-job observation. In order to measure learning effectively, the program designer must understand what behaviors, situations, and exercises will actually simulate the real world. They must then use these activities to measure the learning outcomes.

Our research finds that only 35 percent of programs actually include explicit learning measures. Why is this? For two reasons: first, as I just discussed, it is hard to really measure learning. Second, and even more importantly, learning itself is not always the ultimate goal of many training programs.

In corporate training, learning is a means to an end. Unlike traditional universities and education, where learning results (test scores and grades) are used in an entire context of academic evaluation, corporate training is not really designed to "teach," but rather it is a function that uses "teaching" to improve business performance. Therefore we caution training managers against overusing this as a way of measuring impact. Just remember that in a business environment, the definition of "learning" is very complex: trainers are not really teaching people how to score on a test—trainers are trying to teach people how to perform on the job. Real learning measurement should include on-the-job assessments and measurement of actual job performance under widely changing conditions.

In *The Blended Learning Book*®[3], the concept of "mastery" is defined as a combination of proficiency and retention, driven by experience. "Proficiency" refers to the ability to score well on a test. (For example, after taking the course on Microsoft Excel

Figure 4.7 LSI Logic Learning Objectives
for Field Technical Curriculum

	A	B	C
1	Day 1 Session Objectives		
2	Module	Topic	Trainer
3			
4	Lect:	Product series Family Focus	
5		After completing this module you should be able to:	
6		•Recognize the product series Family	
7		•Identify the upcoming products in the Midrange family	
8	Lect:	ATS Group Overview	
9		After completing this module you should be able to:	
10		•Recognize the roles of the ATS group	
11		•Identify the ATS group for the product and when to contact them	
12			
13		Lab Mission 1: Storage Manager Overview- Planning, Basic Configuration and Partitioning with Maximum Performance	Tech Trainers
14		DS4000 Storage Manager Overview-	Scenario Based
15		•Identify the features and customer benefits of Storage Manager (Why Should the Customer Care)	Verify Data
16		•Navigate through the main menu items and recognize various wizards.	Performance Considerations
17		•Describe the 2 techniques of managing a storage subsystem (in-band and out-of-band)	
18			
19		Planning	
20	Module 1:	• Verify systems and cabling	
21		• Determine number of trays	
22		• Gather IP addresses	
23			
24		Configuring Storage Subsystems with Storage Manager	
25		•Configure storage subsystem capacity into volumes (logical drives) and assign properties	
26		•Recognize how to configure a hot spare drive	
27		•Save configuration profile	
28			
29		Partitioning	
30		•Define partitioning	
31		•Create partitions	
32			
33			
34	Lect:	Hardware Overview:	
35		After completing this module you should be able to:	Show and Tell
36		• Identify disk system components	
37		• Recognize specification differences	
38		• Communicate to the customer the benefits and value of the hardware	
39		• Identify cabling differences	
40		• Discuss the disk systems and drive characteristics.	
41		• Identify Fibre Channel and SATA drive differences	
42		• Identify when to intermix and when not to intermix	
43			
44	Lect:	Product series Competitive Session- PAYG technique	
45		After completing this module you should be able to:	
46		•Identify the advantages of the product series	
47		•Identify the advantages of the unique Dynamic Features	
48		•Recognize the opportunities to grow your sales with Dynamic Features	

pivot tables, I scored 100 percent on the test.) "Retention" refers to the ability to retain and apply such knowledge under changing conditions. (The ability to create pivot tables and use them for large statistical surveys demonstrates this ability.) The "experience curve" is real—it takes time for proficiency and retention to lead to mastery. Training programs that include simulations of the real world try to build this experience quickly. Therefore the measurement of scores as a surrogate for learning only scratches the surface of this area.

Again, our research shows that one-third of organizations regularly measure actual learning—and we believe this is reasonable. Use this measure carefully; it provides excellent actionable information about the program itself, but far less information about the true business impact. Remember that it is the application of learning and its integration into the organization that drive overall business outcomes.

3. Adoption. Adoption is a critically important measure that is sometimes referred to as "butts in seats." While it sounds tactical, it is, in fact, very strategic and actionable.

We define adoption as the percent of the target population who has completed a given program. In a sense, the adoption rate measures indicate how well the program was targeted and marketed, how well the program is being received, and what potential impact the program could have. Many training managers measure the success of a program by the percent of workers who have signed up.

Remember that one of the biggest challenges in corporate training is helping people find the time to prioritize the programs you build. Your "target adoption rate" should be reasonable. It is hard to expect 100 percent of all managers to attend manager training, for example, unless the entire organization considers it mandatory. When adoption rates are very high, it is a strong indication that your program is very highly respected.

Going back to our sales measurement example, in the marketing department, "adoption" is the equivalent to measuring "eyeballs," "website hits," "the number of people who opened a direct-mail piece," or "leads." It measures how well the target audience was actually reached. It does not measure "sales" per se, but it is one of the strongest indicators of sales, and "sales" rarely go up without the number of "leads" or "eyeballs" going up.

An example of how to use adoption measures: Suppose you are launching a leadership development program and the target audience may be all directors and above in the U.S. manufacturing organization. There may be 350 people in this target group. Your goal might be to reach 90 percent of these people within the current fiscal year. By establishing this adoption target (a very aggressive target, by the way), you will now be forced to develop an outreach campaign that may include a series of meetings with executives, various emails from you and the CEO, and scheduled classes that accommodate a wide variety of schedules. If, after the first thirty or sixty days, the adoption rate is low, then you have either a communications, alignment or scheduling problem. Or, worse, the program may have generated a poor reputation.

In some cases adoption measures are the most important ones you have. For example, adoption is a mission-critical measure for compliance programs (such as sexual harassment, safety, or operational quality). For e-learning programs, adoption is the only way you can discern whether learners can find the course and whether or not they are completing. (Completion may or may not be important in an e-learning course, but low completions in a mandatory program are clearly evidence of poor design or a technology problem.)

4. Utility. Utility is a new concept in our model. It is a word used to indicate the "usefulness" of the course to individual learners and their workgroups. It may appear to be a surrogate for an actual performance measure; however, it is actually an indicator[4] of performance, which is much easier to measure than performance itself.

What we found is that "performance" measures are different from "utility" measures. For example, you may find that your favorite screwdriver is a very "useful" tool because it fits your hand well, fits well into most of the screws you have, is easy to fit into your tool chest, is colored easily for you to find, and is strong enough for your tasks. These attributes make it a tool you use frequently and recommend to others. On the job you may not find that you screw screws faster or better with this tool—but you perhaps tighten more screws and use it more frequently because it is so "useful."

In other words, utility measures the "usefulness" of the training program and how easily and regularly you will apply it to your job. A well-designed "time management" course, for example, is considered useful—but may or may not drive improvements in measurable business impact. You clearly want your training programs to score high on this measure.

Utility can easily be measured through surveys and interviews. Survey questions that measure utility include:

- How useful was this course in helping you to improve the efficiency and effectiveness of your current job?
- How well do you feel this course will help you to reduce errors in your current job?
- How strongly would you recommend this course to others in your department?

Note that these questions, while qualitative in nature, were worded to provide you with quantitative indicators by using numeric ranges of answers (see the section on "Best Practices in Implementation"). You can tell that a course is "twice as useful" as another in this way.

5. Efficiency. What is efficiency doing in a measurement model for impact? Considering again that training is a support organization, efficiency measures play a tremendously important role. In fact, according to our usage research, cost is more frequently measured than learning results: almost 40 percent of organizations routinely measure the cost of each training program.

Efficiency measures in a vacuum are not very interesting. But once you start tracking them over time and comparing them to industry benchmarks (such as those in *The Corporate Learning Factbook®*), they are very actionable. These measures help you understand the speed, cost-effectiveness, and resource utilization of program development and delivery.

Efficiency is particularly important for many reasons today. First, remember that perhaps your biggest job as a training manager or executive is resource allocation. A focus on efficiency and the measurement of cost helps you best make these decisions. Some of the important measures that help you here include cost per hour of content development, cost per hour of delivery, and cost per hour of overhead (staff and infrastructure). If you understand the relative efficiency of different types of programs, you can more easily make decisions about which programs to outsource. Program allocation is a critically important decision—and when you decide to outsource a particular function, efficiency measures give you the benchmarks from which to select vendors and decide where your dollars can best be spent.

In addition, if you want to develop a business-focused learning organization, your management wants to make sure that the training budget is being spent in a cost-effective manner. Most training organizations are regularly asking for capital funding for LMS, tools, LCMS, and other investments. As training becomes more of a "shared services" organization and less of a "university," there will be increased scrutiny of your cost of doing business. The CFO may wonder whether a given investment is resulting in lower overall costs and how the "cost per delivered hour" of the training programs compares with others in the industry.[5] You should prepare for this type of analysis and start collecting cost and efficiency data now.

6. Alignment. The term alignment refers to the continuous process of making sure that training investments and programs are focused on the most urgent and critical business problems in the organization. As illustrated in the model, alignment plays an important role across the entire process and can be measured in many ways. We suggest the incorporation of some of alignment measures in the standard evaluations before, during, and after a learning event. Examples of alignment measures include the following:

Investment Alignment

- How well does the program allocation in the training organization reflect the business leaders' perceptions of learning and development needs?
- How well do the training programs align with the organization's broader talent management needs (for instance, the need to recruit and develop more engineers, need to develop mid-line managers, need to increase employee engagement, need to drive a high-performance culture)?
- How well do program managers understand the real business strategies and near-term goals of their assigned business units?

Process Alignment

- How well do the learning and knowledge within this program align with existing business processes (that is, do the processes or programs detailed in the programs match with the reality of how these processes are actually implemented)?
- Are the skills and techniques being taught reinforced through established processes (for instance, are there other tools and systems that agree with and reinforce the materials being taught)?

- Is there a performance plan associated with this learning program? Do managers, for example, understand the need to integrate these learning programs into employee development plans? Is there a way for such integration to take place?

Management Alignment

- How well do line managers and executives understand the value of this particular program? Do they even know about it?
- Do they understand the program's value, where it fits into their business process, who should attend, and the prerequisites?
- Do managers understand the course material itself, so they can reinforce it on the job?
- Will they notify and encourage their employees to attend?

Job Role Alignment

- Are there clearly defined job roles targeted for this program? (For example, are all new managers in production engineering expected to take this course?) We call this element "audience targeting" in *The Blended Learning Book*.
- If so, are the program elements clearly aligned with the job roles and responsibilities as they exist today? For example, are the terminology, grade level, and learning fidelity of the course consistent with the audience being targeted?
- Does the learning program itself have different branches or modules for varying job roles within the same function?
- Is it a part of a certification or learning track for the entire job role? If so, is this certification consistent with the job roles and levels in the organization?

Competency Alignment

- Does the organization have a defined competency model for the individuals targeted for this course? Are there existing competency models used by managers or leaders that the course should build on?

- Are there corporate values or principles that should be incorporated into the program?

- Is the course easy to locate when an individual or manager seeks to develop these competencies? Are there systems or documents that help managers find the right course when faced with a skills gap? (This is particularly complex in large organizations.)

- Does the program develop a set level of proficiency in these competencies that can be applied to a performance or development plan?

- Does the program integrate with the company's performance management system so that completion of the program automatically updates an employee's competency profile or performance plan?

Financial Alignment

- Is this program urgent enough so that managers will agree that it is a good use of the company's resources?

- How well do the learning and development organization's financial priorities align with the priorities in the business units?

- Would a line manager agree that the budget spent on this program is appropriate, given other priorities in his or her organization?

Urgency and Time Alignment

- Are the schedule and time commitment for this course aligned with the pressing and timely business needs in the organization? Are there enough sessions, kiosks, or other materials to let employees take the course without impacting their work environment in a negative way?

- Does the course take too much time away from employees' time on the job?
- Is the self-study requirement too burdensome?

(Some of these issues are covered in the section, "Attainment of Client Objectives.")

As illustrated above, there are many elements of alignment that influence program design, targeting, delivery, and results. We believe alignment must be monitored, tracked, and evaluated to make sure training programs are driving business impact. How this information is actually captured is discussed in the following section.

7. Attainment of Client Objectives (Customer Satisfaction). This measure is one of the most important of all: "customer satisfaction." How well were the specific business requirements of the business user or manager met, whatever they may be? In some cases, the key customer goal is to deliver the program on-time and on-budget. In other cases the customer goal is to reach 100 percent completion by a certain date. In the Six Sigma methodology (discussed later), this is called the "voice of the customer"—and is often considered the most important measure of all. (See Chapter 8: Attainment: Measurement of Customer Satisfaction.)

8. Individual Performance. The term "individual performance" refers to the individual job performance of each learner who attended the program. This measure equates well to Kirkpatrick's Level 3. How do you get a sense of individual performance improvements? First, if the program manager did an excellent job of performance consulting (needs analysis), the training manager will have specific job-level measures that can be impacted by the program. For example, if you are assigned to develop a program to "train the sales force in product A" you should try to establish "What is the volume of sales of Product A now?" and "What do you believe the improvement should be, after this course?" These questions can be answered in a well-designed "Business Unit Signoff Form" that we will discuss in the implementation section of this book.

We urge you to consider establishing these goals up-front—during the performance consulting process. It is at this point that you have the most attention from line management, and you can easily establish some sense of the magnitude of the performance problems and potential measurable improvements in the process. By doing this before program design, you can use these performance goals to help guide program development, and you have instant credibility when you start to measure results.

Another way to measure individual performance improvement is through your organization's performance management process. While this is far more subjective, if you have a close relationship with the business units sponsoring the training, you may be able to build program elements that correspond directly to performance goals in performance plans.

An excellent example of this is the measurement process used by Randstad in their onboarding program. Randstad is one of the world's largest temporary employment agencies, so their onboarding program is widely used by almost every new "employee." The training organization has aligned the training program directly with the performance expectations of new hires during their first one or two years. (This process is discussed in Chapter 6: Measurement of Business Impact.) The Randstad case study is in Appendix I: Case Study A: Randstad Measures Onboarding.) If you are building a "talent-driven" program that integrates with onboarding, or leadership development, for example, it may be easy to identify specific employee performance goals your training can focus on. These will be easy to measure because they are already captured in the company's performance management process. (For example, "employees who attended the 'strategic planning process' course were rated

32 percent higher in 'strategic thinking' in their performance appraisals than those who did not.")

9. Organizational Performance. Ultimately, the goal of any training program is to improve organizational performance (or overall business metrics). This measure is similar to Kirkpatrick's Level 4. Organizational performance may or may not derive directly from individual performance, by the way. This measure is the most difficult to capture because it is never directly linked to a training program.

In fact, one of the things I have found in my numerous discussions with training and HR managers is that often the ultimate benefits of well-built training programs are more cultural than the organizations realized.

For example, at Scottrade, the company developed a very focused online simulation program to help new sales representatives understand how to qualify and promote Scottrade's services. The program is highly interactive, entertaining, and very business focused. As the program manager rolled out the program, they found that it did, in fact, dramatically improve the quality of leads being generated and the number of new accounts.

However, in addition to this result, this program had several other benefits. First, the sales organization reported that sales representatives were happier, more enthusiastic, more confident, and more engaged. Retention levels were higher. And when Scottrade started to describe the program to candidates, the hiring rates went up.

These types of benefits, while hard to measure, have huge organizational impact. Some of the common "unexpected" benefits of excellent development programs include:

- Increased level of **employee engagement** (which can be measured through Gallup Q12 and other employee survey tools)

- Increased level of **retention,** driven by higher confidence in their job roles (a measure that most organizations already capture and one that can easily be quantified)

- Increased level of **flexibility and mobility** in the workforce, driven by employees' understanding that the company is both (a) investing in them and (b) making it easier for them to succeed in new roles

- Improvement in **hiring rates,** driven by job candidates' desire to be part of an organization that will give them development opportunities and coaching to succeed

- Improvement in the organization's **employment brand,** its market image as an employer. This brand has tremendous impact on the ability of the company to attract and select high-powered people.

While these types of benefits cannot always be tied to a performance-driven learning program, they can easily be tied to an onboarding, management development, leadership development, or career development program. Their financial benefits are very large (typically 10 to 100X the cost of the program). Also, if you are in an organization that feels the need to measure impact very carefully, many of these types of measures are already being captured by your HR organization.

What about ROI? As I said earlier in this book, we do not recommend using ROI to measure organizational performance. Let us explain why through an example from NCR.

An excellent example of the complexity of measuring organizational performance is a field-service training program that was carefully measured by NCR. The company has a field-service force, which maintains and repairs a wide range of computing and IT systems throughout the world. NCR has a series of in-depth certification programs for service technicians.

NCR decided to evaluate this program and used the typical ROI method. In the ROI analysis, the NCR program director decided that the best measure of individual performance would be time to repair (TTR) for individuals who attended the program versus those who did not. Presumably, those technicians who were certified should have shorter TTR measures than those who were not certified.

NCR captured TTR data across a large sample of certified and non-certified technicians, and analyzed the data. The company found that those technicians who were certified and scored well on their certification program (that is, scored high in Kirkpatrick's Level 2) were, in fact, taking longer to repair equipment than those who were not certified. It appeared that "individual performance" was not leading to an improvement in "organizational performance."

NCR also found that, in fact, the measurement process was flawed. The reason that TTR was higher for certified technicians was that managers were so impressed with the skills of the trained personnel that they were sending them to work on the hardest service problems—so of course the TTR for certified technicians was longer.

This example is included here only to illustrate some of the challenges in trying to measure ROI as an organizational performance measure. While it is an important option, we warn managers that, in many cases, this particular measure will be the most suspect and difficult to correlate to training; so we do not recommend focusing overly on trying to measure ROI as a measurement of training programs unless there is strong alignment with line management. Organizational performance will "derive" from training in many interesting and often unpredictable ways.

As discussed in Chapter 6: Measurement of Business Impact, the best way to measure organizational performance is to monitor business metrics that are already being captured.

Summary of the Framework

Figure 4.8 shows the nine measurement areas in an easier-to-read format. Satisfaction and learning, which are well understood by most learning managers and are most frequently measured, are shown at the top. Individual and organizational performance, which are the more difficult and less frequently used measures, are shown at the bottom.

To summarize, Figure 4.9 gives examples of specific measures for each measurement area.

Program Versus Organizational Measures

The nine measures in the Learning Impact Measurement Framework are program-level indicators as well as organization-level

Figure 4.8 The Nine Impact Framework Measurement Areas

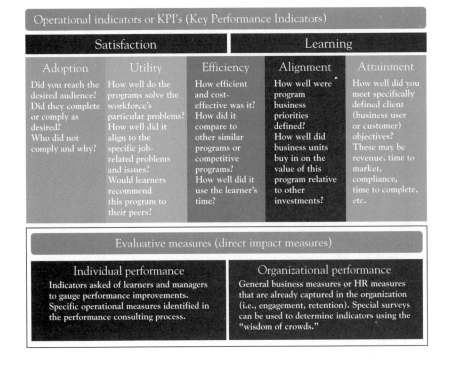

Figure 4.9 Examples of the Nine Impact Measurement Areas

Measurement area	Description	Specific examples and actionable results
Satisfaction	How satisfied are the learners with the program and learning experience?	Satisfaction is a very powerful and multidimensional measure. While it directly indicates the quality of the program and learning experience, well-crafted satisfaction measures can give indicators of utility, alignment, and attainment.
Learning	• How well did the audience achieve the learning objectives? • Did the learners "pass" the course? • Can the learners apply the skills and knowledge on the job?	Learning measures directly track achievement of the program's learning objectives. In the context of business value, learning measures are a "means to an end." For many programs (e.g., compliance and certification) that are well-aligned, learning outcomes are excellent measures of business impact. Beware of widely promoting learning results as business impact, however – if the program is not well-aligned and well-adopted, learning may not have much meaning to line-of-business managers.
Adoption	How well was the program adopted by the target audience?	Adoption measures how well the program was targeted and marketed to its intended audience. Adoption delivers critical feedback to help training managers understand how well the intended audience was reached. Why was the adoption rate low? How can the right learners be better targeted? Is role-specific or job-specific training needed? Are managers engaged in the process?
Utility	How useful is the course to the audience?	Utility is the learner's and manager's perception of on-the-job value. How well does the course meet specific job objectives? How well does it meet the performance improvement objectives set up-front? Would learners recommend this course to others? (This measure is very similar to "job impact" in the Kirkpatrick model.)
Efficiency	How much did this course cost to develop, deliver, and take?	Efficiency is a critical measure for excellence in the training organization. Was this course developed and delivered in the most efficient way? How much did it really cost? How do these costs compare against other similar programs?
Alignment	How well does this course align with current urgent business problems?	Alignment crosses all four phases of the business impact model. How well do line managers buy in on the value of this course? How well does this course fit into the overall corporate priorities? (See "case in point: Caterpillar's planning and budgeting process" and "case in point: CNA insurance training investment model.") How well do managers support the learners in implementing the processes and procedures taught in the training? What percent of the programs in the training plan are considered "strategic"? At an individual level, alignment refers to how well the program aligns to the needs of its audience. Did the people who attended have the right levels of basic prerequisite skills? Did they have the support of their managers? Did the attendees come to the course fully motivated and enabled to learn what was needed?
Attainment of customer objectives	How well does this course meet the customer's stated objectives?	How well does this course meet the "voice-of-the-customer" needs? If it is a compliance course, does it meet the compliance guidelines? Was it delivered on-time? Was it delivered on-time? Was the quality what the business owner wanted?
Individual performance	How well did the program increase the individual measurable performance of the learners?	Individual performance can be tied directly to the root-cause analysis identified in the performance consulting phase. If a quantifiable business problem is identified up-front and this is detailed into a root-cause, this measure can be monitored before and after training. If the organization has a well-implemented performance management process, data from performance reviews can also be correlated to training.
Organizational performance	How well did the program drive total business or workgroup impact?	While it is ultimately the most important measure of all, organizational performance is the most difficult to measure directly and often leads to conclusions that can be challenged by business managers. Techniques and case studies for organizational performance measurement are included in this report.

indicators. In the beginning, companies may start measuring these areas at a program level. Over time, however, as more and more programs are measured in a repeatable way, the overall adoption, utility, efficiency, alignment, and attainment measures across the organization as a whole can be measured.

For example, at Depository Trust Clearing Corporation (DTCC) the organization believes strongly in the Six Sigma approach to measurement. They established a set of measures that are used to measure attainment of customer satisfaction. "On-time delivery" (measured in days late) is one of these measures. The organization scores each learning program on its "on-time delivery" metric and compares that against the "on-time delivery" average for all programs.

Other Important Operational Measures. In addition to the impact measures discussed, almost all training organizations measure a variety of operational indicators that monitor the operation of the training function itself. These include the measures of production, efficiency, job satisfaction, and impact of the training organization.

Typical measures include:

- **Volume**—Hours of training delivered, hours per training head count, hours per employee;
- **Economic efficiency**—Total spending per hour delivered, total spending per employee in training, total spending per employee;
- **Time-based measures**—Time to build a course, time from product launch to training availability;
- **Quality measures**—Number of bugs in courses, number of technical support calls;
- **Utilization measures**—Total enrollments, total completions, percent utilization of the course catalog, percent utilization of facilities and instructors; and

- **Team satisfaction measures**—Job satisfaction in the learning organization.

While there are many more, these are measures to be established as part of the operational strategy. These measures should be used by a "learning services organization" to provide actionable information about how to improve the effectiveness and efficiency of the learning organization.[6]

How to Use the Measurement Framework

This Impact Measurement Framework is intended to be used for two purposes. First, it offers a way to help you categorize and prioritize what should be measured. It should free you from the limitations of the Kirkpatrick model. No organization measures every one of the areas in detail, but any high-impact learning organization should measure some of these. All nine of these measurement areas are business-oriented, actionable, and fairly easy to measure.

Second, the framework should provide a way to simplify the measurement process. By understanding the concepts behind each of these measurement areas (including satisfaction and learning, which, as assumed, will always be measured), assessments, evaluations, or processes to measure each can be easily implemented. We have tried to define them in a clear way with many examples of ways to measure each.

Summary of the Measurement Models

Figure 4.10 provides a summary of the Kirkpatrick and Bersin measures with specific examples of how and where each measure can be used. In this chart, "individual" and "organizational" performances are grouped together.

Figure 4.10 Summary of Measurement Areas

Measure	Good for	Best process to use				Comments
		End of course evaluations	LMS captured information	Financial systems and tools	Qualitative interviews and analysis	
Satisfaction (Kirkpatrick)	Course quality, experience, instructor, facility.	Excellent	No	No	Yes, qualitative comments and interviews are highly valuable.	Satisfaction measures should always be captured to get feedback on quality and learning experience.
Learning (Kirkpatrick)	Determining if learning objectives are met, instructional design quality.	Excellent	No	No	No	Learning results are important but usually embodied in impact and effectiveness measures. Can be very valuable to instructional design process.
Adoption	Determining alignment and how well the program is integrated into business and performance planning processes.	No	Yes	No	No	Important measure for any e-learning program, any compliance program, and any corporatewide program to understand why the program is or is not being used.
Utility	Determining how well the program meets the performance consulting objectives defined in advance.	Excellent	No	No	Yes, qualitative interviews with learners and managers are critical here.	Utility is a broader term than job impact. This measure is intended to understand how well the program solves the stated performance problem, and how well the learners can and do apply the learning to their work.
Efficiency	Determines cost-effectiveness of program, whether media was appropriate, and how well the program scaled.	No	Yes, somewhat	Yes, a cost-accounting based system is needed to determine these measures.	No	Important measures to a learning services organization, typical measures would be cost to build, cost per student hour, development time versus delivery time (ratio), reuse percentage, etc.
Alignment	Determines how well performance consulting process was delivered, how well the program was prioritized and how engaged the training organization is with lines of business.	Manager evaluations	No	No	Yes, qualitative interviews with managers and executives are vital.	Important measures to determine how strategic this program is considered by line managers, how much impact learners believe it has, and how well it competes with other training and HR investments.
Attainment of client objectives	Critical measure of customer satisfaction, as defined by the business owner.	Yes	Yes	Yes	Yes	These are measures defined by the customer – they may be on-time delivery, cost, time in class, satisfaction level, or other. Very important to maintaining a service-level agreement with business units.
Total business impact or ROI	Can be used for large programs where investment is large and often questioned.	No	No	Yes. Requires establishing base metrics before training and measuring again after training.	Yes	To make these measures believable, the organization must clearly define some metrics before and after training, and then use learner assessments or control groups to correlate these changes to training. Not recommended for regular use.

Notes

1. For a detailed discussion of all the options for the design of blended-learning programs, we recommend Josh Bersin's *The Blended Learning Book: Best Practices, Proven Methodologies, and Lessons Learned*. San Francisco, CA: Pfeiffer, 2004.

2. For more information, see *High-Impact Talent Management: Trends, Best Practices, and Industry Solutions*. Bersin & Associates/ Josh Bersin, May 2007. Available at www.bersin.com.

3. For more information, see Josh Bersin's *The Blended Learning Book: Best Practices, Proven Methodologies, and Lessons Learned*. San Francisco, CA: Pfeiffer, 2004.

4. An "indicator" is a measure that is easy to capture and gives information that can be asserted or correlated to business performance.

5. For more information, see *The Corporate Learning Factbook® 2007: Statistics, Benchmarks and Analysis of the U.S. Corporate Training Market*. Bersin & Associates/Karen O'Leonard, February 2007. Available at www.bersin.com.

6. For more information, see The High-Impact Learning Organization: WhatWorks® in *The Management, Organization, and Governance of Corporate Training*. Bersin & Associates, June 2005. Available at www.bersin.com.

Chapter Five

Implementation: The Seven-Step Training Measurement Process

Now that we have carefully discussed our approach to measurement, the impact model, and the nine measurement areas available, your mind is probably asking "How do I apply all these new ideas?" This chapter moves directly into practical reality. It examines the nuts and bolts of measurement from a program perspective, based on the best practices we have identified from discussions with dozens of organizations.

The Seven-Step Program Measurement Process

After talking with hundreds of companies, we have identified seven independent steps, shown in Figure 5.1, involved in the training measurement process. While you may or may not choose to use every step, it is valuable to understand and consider each.

Step 1: Business Unit Signoff

As we discussed in Chapter 2, before beginning a program there is an important phase of "problem identification." Before even this takes place, however, training managers must make sure they are fully aligned with the business. My personal belief is that training is at its core a business process, not a learning process. The learning that takes place in training is a means to an end—and the "end" is defined by business managers.

Figure 5.1 The Seven Steps to Program Measurement

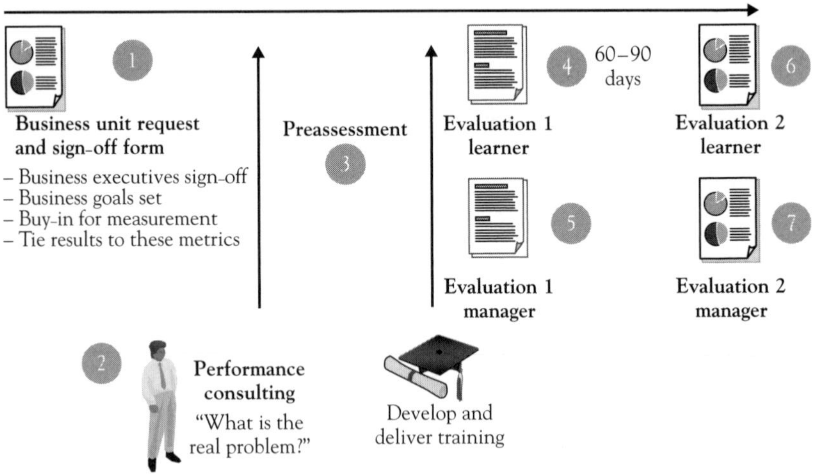

Therefore, if you want to stay aligned and business-focused, the first step in the development of a training program is to clearly identify the size, scope, and nature of the problem to be solved. We often call this process "performance consulting" (often referred to as "needs analysis" or "root-cause analysis").

In most companies, performance consulting starts when someone runs into the room and tells you about a problem. "We are not selling enough product A!" or "We are having quality problems in process B!" Your immediate reaction, of course, is to jump into action.

But how do you know whether this particular problem is the most important one to work on? How do you know that the manager asking for help is well aligned with other problems in his or her workgroup or functional organization? How do you know that the problem he or she is worried about today is not temporary and may go away on its own?

The only way to answer these questions is to gain business alignment early. One important technique to doing this is the

"Business Unit Signoff Form." This form should be filled in by the business manager requesting training support and should include several pieces of information, including:

- A description of the business problem to be addressed, stated in business terms (for instance, we are 35 percent below plan in sales of product A);
- The financial size or quantified loss (or potential gain, if solved) for this problem (for instance, this is costing us $10M per quarter in lost sales);
- Time deadlines for solving this problem (for instance, we must solve this problem by the end of the year);
- Budget allocated by the business unit to solve the problem (if any);
- Audience to be reached—its size, nature, and other issues that must be considered in reaching this audience; and
- Signoff by the manager, director, and vice president of the business unit requesting the training.

If you do not have such a signoff form, you should develop one immediately. It offers you many valuable tools for alignment and measurement:

- First, it ensures that the executives in the business agree on the nature of the problem, its scope, and its priority.
- Second, it forces the line-of-business manager to quantify the size of the problem. This is the first step in performance consulting. Now, when the time comes to measure business impact, you have a clear understanding of the nature of the problem to be solved, stated in terms the business understands.
- Third, it provides information to help prioritize competing requests for training. If one department wants a program to

solve a $100,000 problem and another has a problem that is believed to be a $10 million problem, you have a clear and easy way to go back to the first manager and explain why his program is not your top priority.

- Fourth, it helps you to scope the solution and start to define your budget and strategy. You have a sense of the size of the problem, nature of the audience, and relative effort required.

- Finally, it helps you gain alignment and adoption during the rollout phase. If the business has signed off on the program (at a high level), you should have no problems getting people to attend the program.

Some organizations take this process even further. They give the business manager some guidelines for selecting/recommending the nature of training they desire: should the course be instructor-led, e-learning, or a job aid (for instance, at FedEx Kinko's many of the training interventions are job aids, showing employees how to fix copiers, produce documents, and so on). Ideally, these decisions should be made during the solution development phase, but often managers have a clear reason for specifying a delivery approach based on the problem they are experiencing.

Figure 5.2 is an example of a simple, but effective, signoff form, developed by Randstad.

Step 2: Performance Consulting

The second phase of measurement is the performance consulting phase. Performance consulting is a needs-assessment process that must be completed to identify the root cause of the business problem. (In our High-Impact Learning Organization® research[1], it was found that this is the single biggest driver of high-impact learning programs.) For this discussion, performance consulting is the process of working with the line of business to diagnose the business problem and assess the needs, and then working with instructional

Figure 5.2 Business Unit Signoff Form

Curriculum Project Request and High Level Design

Project owner's name:

Department:

Business problem:

Strategic alignment:

Desired business impact: (improvements in revenue, gross margin, improved retention, decreased risk, etc)

Impact of training: (improvement estimated due to training)

Estimated implementation date:

Target audience:
Audience job role:

High level overview of learning solution:
Performance objectives:

Contact time:
Delivery approach:
Facilitation approach:

Total expense:
Estimated development expense:
Estimated delivery expense:
Estimated salary expense of participants:

Approval signatures

Sponsoring managing director:

Project owner:

Chief learning officer:

MD who oversees target audience:

MD who oversees target audience:

MD who oversees target audience:

Source: Randstad (2006)

designers to develop, launch, manage, and assess the training solution. Performance consulting does not presume that the solution is training. (See Figure 5.3.)

Why is this step considered Step 2 of the measurement process? If you want to maintain alignment and efficiency in your programs, you should measure compliance with this critical step.

Figure 5.3 The Performance Consulting Process

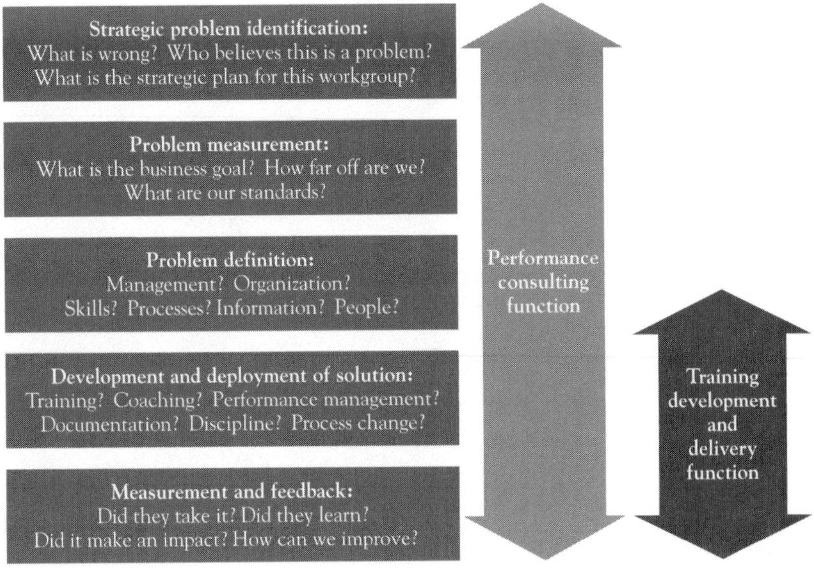

Some organizations require training managers to fill out specific forms that describe the problems being identified, often following a "root cause analysis" tree. The form may, for example, ask the program manager to explain the specific diagnosis used to determine the learning problem at hand. It may ask the manager to explain why the problem is not necessarily one of process design or management (which often evidence themselves as perceived learning problems). These forms force the program manager to diagnose the problem in a clear and explicit way. These critical business problems are then included in the "dashboard" of programs that describes the training programs to the rest of the organization. Figure 5.4 shows such a form.

In addition, the performance consulting process itself will capture many of the measures you can then use later to gauge results. Consider the following example:

A large retailer had a problem with increasing the sales of its high-margin electronics products. Rather than rush out and start

Figure 5.4 Measurement as Part of Performance Consulting

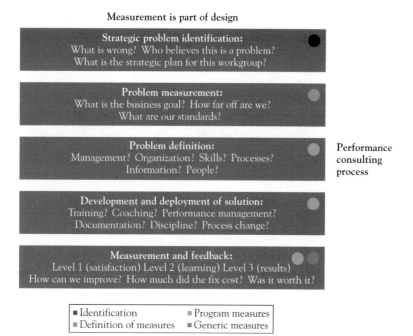

Measurement is part of design

Strategic problem identification:
What is wrong? Who believes this is a problem?
What is the strategic plan for this workgroup?

Problem measurement:
What is the business goal? How far off are we?
What are our standards?

Problem definition:
Management? Organization? Skills? Processes?
Information? People?

Development and deployment of solution:
Training? Coaching? Performance management?
Documentation? Discipline? Process change?

Measurement and feedback:
Level 1 (satisfaction) Level 2 (learning) Level 3 (results)
How can we improve? How much did the fix cost? Was it worth it?

Performance consulting process

■ Identification   ■ Program measures
■ Definition of measures ■ Generic measures

to build product sales training, the company's performance consultant worked with the store managers to identify the behaviors of highly successful sales representatives. The consultant realized that the root cause of the "lower sales" was not only lack of product knowledge, but also the behavior of sales representatives. (This is sometimes called "critical mistake analysis.")

The consultant identified the five most important things to "fix" to increase high-margin product sales. As remedies, the organization needed to be certain that each sales representative:

• Can answer questions correctly;

• Understands what equipment the customer already has, so he or she could recommend the right high-technology add-on product;

- Does not mention or recommend a product that is out of stock;
- Does not let a customer handle a nonworking demonstration model; and
- Does not ignore a customer who is browsing around the store.

Once these five critical "root causes" of the problem were identified, it was easy to put together a program (with mystery shoppers) to measure the change in these five indicators. The organization implemented the training solution and monitored behavior in these five areas over time—iterating on the program to make sure it delivered on these sales performance indicators. Today, this training program is an integral part of new-hire training and new product training at this organization.

There is an important lesson here. The root-cause analysis done during performance consulting identified both the learning objectives as well as the performance indicators. This allowed the training organization to measure the critical business indicators without trying to measure sales improvement. You should standardize your performance consulting process to look for these kinds of indicators in every single training program you develop.

Step 3: Pre-Assessment

The third step available to you is pre-assessment. There are many possible reasons for pre-assessment. It may be useful to develop a customized "prescriptive" program that varies from learner to learner. It may be useful to measure "improvements in learning" from before to after a course. And in other cases it may be used to let learners themselves decide whether the course is even worth taking. While it is not necessary or frequently used for most training programs, it is something you should consider—especially when you have a high-volume program.

Let us look again at Randstad's onboarding program. Thousands of staff go through this program each year. To help the training organization understand the changing nature of new employee needs, every new employee takes a pre-assessment before attending this program. This helps Randstad continuously monitor skills gaps among employee groups over time. At the end of the program, each learner takes a post-assessment. Randstad then computes the percent increase in this metric as a way of measuring how their instructors are doing, specifically, and how well the program, in general, is meeting the needs of its ever-changing temporary workforce.

An example of how Randstad generalizes this strategy is shown in Figure 5.5.

In this example, Randstad measures the delta (change) between pre- and post-assessments across a large number of new employees. Since the company has been collecting this information for many years, they can see when the delta (improvement) gets higher or lower. When the delta gets low, they know the program needs

Figure 5.5 Randstad Pre- Versus Post-Assessment Process

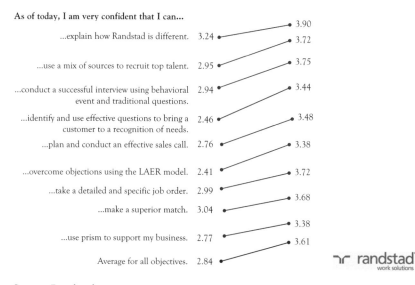

As of today, I am very confident that I can...

...explain how Randstad is different.	3.24	3.90
		3.72
...use a mix of sources to recruit top talent.	2.95	3.75
...conduct a successful interview using behavioral event and traditional questions.	2.94	3.44
...identify and use effective questions to bring a customer to a recognition of needs.	2.46	3.48
...plan and conduct an effective sales call.	2.76	3.38
...overcome objections using the LAER model.	2.41	3.72
...take a detailed and specific job order.	2.99	
		3.68
...make a superior match.	3.04	
		3.38
...use prism to support my business.	2.77	3.61
Average for all objectives.	2.84	

randstad
work solutions

Source: Randstad

work. This helps the company determine several actionable, important things about this program, including the following.

- How well was a particular session conducted?
- Is this particular incoming group more savvy than others?
- Is the nature of the incoming workforce changing?
- Does the company need to revamp the program because of changes in skills in the incoming workforce?

When using a pre-assessment, the results of an end-of-course assessment do not have to be "normalized." A target learning objective can be set to measure not only the final scores but also the percent increase in scores from beginning to end. This approach normalizes the effect of different employees coming to the course with different levels of knowledge.

Even so, pre-assessments should be reserved for high-value, high-volume courses. While they seem useful, they dramatically increase the training manager's workload. In order to be useful, the pre-assessment must be:

- Developed as part of the learning plan;
- Tested to make sure it accurately reflects the audience's skills and knowledge; and
- Tied carefully to the post-program assessment to make sure that the two are directly linked to the same learning objectives.

New-hire training, new manager training, mandatory sales training, and other high-volume programs are good candidates for pre-assessments.

Step 4: Evaluation 1 for the Learner

Step 4 is the standard end-of-course evaluation. If you do nothing else, you must do this. A standardized, well-developed learner evaluation is the most important element in training measurement.

Consider a set of questions that captures the business impact measures in Bersin & Associates Learning Impact Measurement Framework. Consider the following: at the end of a course, the best information to capture is the learner's opinions and general assessments about value. This is the point in time when the learner feels the most immediate "pain" or "gain" from the program. If you carefully develop questions that have numeric values and can be reused across all programs, these measures will be highly varied from program to program and audience to audience, making them actionable.

One example of a standard end-of-course evaluation is the one shown in Figure 5.6, which was developed at HP. This evaluation is designed to fit into HP's measurement framework (see Appendix II: Case Study B: HP Develops an Integrated Measurement Process).

Some of the important measurement areas to consider in the end-of-course survey include:

- Satisfaction and free text feedback on course logistics, materials, instructor, and facilities (satisfaction and course quality measures);

- Relevance of the material to the learner's job and the problem he or she needs to solve (utility measures);

- Whether the learner would recommend the course to other employees in similar jobs (utility and impact measures);

- Whether the time spent on this course was worthwhile (alignment and efficiency measures) when compared with other development opportunities;

- How well the learner's manager supported the course and why he or she took the course (alignment measure); and

- How well the course met the learner's personal objectives for the program, as well as the stated objectives (effectiveness and quality measure).

Figure 5.6 HP Standard End-of-Course Survey

Workforce Development and Organization Effectiveness
FY'05 Classroom ILT Course Evaluation

i n v e n t

Instructions: Please be sure to fill in the information fields provided below, as well as the demographics of Level, Region, Business and Vendor, as all are critical information for reporting purposes.

Fill in bubbles like this: ●
To change a response,
cross it out and mark another.

Demographics

Course Name: ▮▮▮   Date: ▯▯▯▯▯▯ . 2 0 0 5

Course Number: ▯▯▯   Your Name: (optional) ▯▯▯

Instructor: ▯▯▯   Vendor: ▯▯▯

Location: ▯▯▯   **Business:** ○ TSG   ○ Worldwide Operations
                                                ○ CSG   ○ Infrastructure
Level: ○ Individual Contributor (IC) ○ IC Leading a Project Team ○ Manager   ○ IPG   ○ Channel Partner
Region: ○ Americas   ○ Asia - Pacific   ○ EMEA   ○ Japan   ○ PSG   ○ Non-HP Employee

Course Feedback

	Strongly Disagree	Disagree	Neutral	Agree	Strongly Agree
1. The training techniques used to teach the different skills/concepts maximized my learning.	○	○	○	○	○
2. The skills/concepts taught are highly relevant to the demands of my job/role.	○	○	○	○	○
3. The instructor(s) style, methods, and pace helped me to learn.	○	○	○	○	○
4. What I have learned will significantly enhance my job/role performance.	○	○	○	○	○
5. I feel strongly motivated to apply these new skills/concepts in my job/role.	○	○	○	○	○
6. I believe that this program achieved its stated objectives.	○	○	○	○	○
7. I would highly recommend this learning solution to my peers.	○	○	○	○	○

8. I would describe my overall satisfaction with the logistics supporting this course to be:

○ Dissatisfied   ○ Somewhat Dissatisfied   ○ Somewhat Satisfied   ○ Satisfied   ○ Completely Satisfied

9. I would describe my overall level of satisfaction with the instruction provided in the course to be:

○ Dissatisfied   ○ Somewhat Dissatisfied   ○ Somewhat Satisfied   ○ Satisfied   ○ Completely Satisfied

10. I would describe my overall satisfaction with the program content to be:

○ Dissatisfied   ○ Somewhat Dissatisfied   ○ Somewhat Satisfied   ○ Satisfied   ○ Completely Satisfied

11. I would rate the quality of this learning solution to be: ○ Poor   ○ Fair   ○ Good   ○ Very Good   ○ Excellent

12. What comments do you have about any aspect of the course (instructor, content, etc.)?

Source: Hewlett-Packard Corporation

Do not focus solely on satisfaction measures. These miss a major opportunity to gain important business impact and alignment information.

How can an organization ensure that the learner completes the survey? Here are a few tricks. First, make sure the learners complete the survey during a period of time near the end of the course, and don't let them leave until it is completed. Second, just do not give the learners a completion status until the surveys are fully completed and returned.

Step 5: Evaluation 1 for the Manager

The next step in the seven-step process is one that is rarely used but can be a very valuable way to measure impact and alignment: a survey or interview of the learner's manager.

The learner's manager provides a very different perspective and much more unbiased "impact level" feedback than the learner. Remember, the manager truly "pays the bills" for the course by letting the employee attend. He or she has the greatest vested interest in giving honest and direct feedback on value.

Manager evaluations should be delivered a week or more after the course is completed, so the manager has time to talk with his or her employee. Ask the manager a set of questions similar to the learner's questions, but focused on the manager's perception of value, for example:

How worthwhile was this course for your employee in increasing his or her on-the-job performance?

(A) Excellent use of his/her time;

(B) Good use of his/her time;

(C) Useful, but may not be the best use of his/her time;

(D) Marginal use of his/her time; or

(E) Not worth his/her time.

The purpose of these questions is to force the manager to evaluate the usefulness, value, and overall impact of the program. Remember to let the manager write in comments and, when receiving comments, call the manager to obtain his or her direct feedback.

Direct interviews will tell you many things that may not come out clearly in feedback forms. A simple conversation with three to five managers will often provide as much insight as a large number of surveys.

Step 6: Follow-Up Evaluation for the Learner (Optional)

A valuable step (although optional) used by organizations for some programs is a follow-up survey directed to the learner. The purpose of this second evaluation is to learn about actual job and business impact. After an employee has had the opportunity to spend sixty to ninety days on the job, he or she can look back and get a better sense of the value provided by the program. If the company is investing in a high-cost, high-value program (for example, onboarding, professional certification), this type of feedback will give you valuable information about the utility of various course elements and topics.

For this follow-up evaluation, consider questions like:

- How much value did this training have on your ability to complete your job?
- Now that you have had time to apply the principles in this course, how valuable were the lessons in Chapter 1, 2, 3? (Then use a 1 to 5 scale to calibrate and range the responses.)
- If you think about your performance improvements in the last several months, what percent improvement in your job performance do you believe was attributable to this training?
- Considering now how you have applied this course toward your job, which elements of the program were the most valuable? Which had the least value? (List them, since the learner may not remember them at this point.)
- Now that you have had time to apply the materials from this course, what do you now feel was missing from this program? How could you have improved the program?

Although the response rate for these surveys will be much lower (probably one-half to one-third the response rate from the standard end-of-course evaluations), the data will be even more valuable for impact assessment.

Step 7: Follow-Up Evaluation for the Manager (Optional)

Finally, another optional step is to deliver a follow-up evaluation to the manager. Again, this will provide unfiltered information on the true value of the program. After sixty to ninety days, managers will have even more on-the-job feedback on the value of the training and what, if any, impact it has had on their workgroup's performance. To make this type of evaluation actionable, ask specific questions about how behaviors have changed in areas that were covered in the training.

Best Practices in Implementation

These seven steps make up the prototypical best practice measurement program. Do all companies undertake each of these steps? No. Our research shows that only 78 percent of organizations even perform any end-of-course evaluation, and very few undertake manager and follow-up surveys. Here are some tips learned from the organizations we studied.

Make End-of-Course Evaluations Mandatory

A simple, easy-to-implement process is to make end-of-course evaluations mandatory. Many organizations (for example, Children's Hospital of Philadelphia) do not give course credit unless and until the learner has completed the end-of-course survey.

To make the evaluations easy to complete, make sure that every program (including e-learning programs) has time built in for survey completion. Attendees want to give feedback—give them time to do it thoughtfully.

If the program is long (for example, multi-day), also consider having separate evaluations for each day—with a final "standardized" end–of-course evaluation on the final day. Attendees will often forget the "good" and "bad" parts of the program after a few days, and the organization will want to capture attendees' feelings as soon as possible.

Make Evaluations Easy But Meaningful

The end-of-course evaluation (see section, "Steps to Getting Started") should not be too long. Typically you should include only one or two pages of meaningful and thoughtful questions. Simplistic questions (for example, "How did you like this course?") do not provide actionable information nor do they motivate the learner to think hard about how the course could be improved. (Review some of the questions in HP's end-of-course survey in the figure above for examples.)

Give learners many opportunities to offer suggestions. Just as well-run restaurants and retailers give customers suggestion forms, the end-of-course evaluation process should encourage learners to provide specific, detailed suggestions. Give the learners space to write in comments, and make sure all the comments for each program and each session of the program are carefully scanned.

Collect Session- and Time-Specific Information

A simple but sometimes overlooked process is to make sure that each evaluation contains information about the particular session, instructor, location, date, and time of the training. This information can identify problems with a particular facility or instructor.

Try Not to Make Evaluations Anonymous

There is no reason to make evaluations anonymous. Unless the company has some policy against employee feedback, the name, location, job role, level, and contact information of the learners are vitally important when analyzing the evaluations. It may turn out, for example, that experienced employees find a particular program less valuable than new employees. This important piece of information gives you the insight to create a second version of the course, more advanced, for more senior employees. (There is an argument that someone may give more honest feedback if it is anonymous. We have found that people who provide positive feedback give their names freely, whereas, negative feedback is often provided anonymously.)

Collect as Much Other Dimensional Information as Possible

Descriptive information about the audience or program is often called "dimensional" information in an analytics system. Much of this dimensional information is available via the LMS or should be captured in the end-of-course evaluation. Examples of dimensional information include:

- Course name, version, session ID, date, time, instructor;
- Location of course, facility, room;
- Learner name, job title, level, years of seniority;
- For an e-learning course—the final score, completion rate, number of pages viewed, time spent in the course; and
- Details about course delivery, such as:
  - Were handouts given?
  - Were job aids given?
  - Which version of content was used?

Use the LMS for Evaluation, If Possible

Use the LMS evaluation tool, if possible, to collect information directly; this reduces the possibility of error and greatly simplifies the process of analyzing the data after it is collected. Organizations will often have students use an online terminal or PC to complete surveys in the classroom after the course is completed.

At Randstad, for example, the LMS evaluation process is integrated into the course enrollment and launch process. The LMS then reminds learners and managers when they have not yet completed an evaluation. An example from Randstad's LMS is shown in Figure 5.7.

Bring Managers into the Process

Help managers take ownership of the process. If management sponsored the program (through the completion of the signoff form), they will be interested in the outcome. Line management is ultimately responsible for making sure that employees take

Figure 5.7 Randstad's Use of the LMS for Measurement

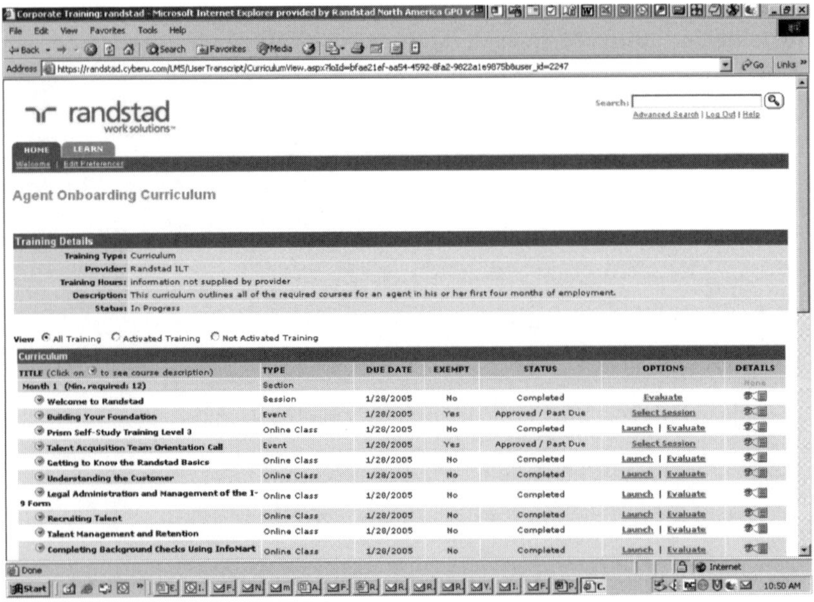

Source: Randstad

training seriously. Therefore, enlist the help of line management to make sure evaluations are completed. (You may want to tell managers that their employees will not receive credit until the evaluation forms are completed.)

At HP, for example, standard end-of-course evaluations provide a wide range of metrics. These evaluations are used within the training organization to improve program development and delivery. Then they are converted into color-coded scorecards that are sent directly to line managers, so they can see the results of the training in which their people participated. By delivering summaries in a form that managers want to see, HP makes sure that their employees complete evaluations and then discusses the results of training with them directly.

Integrate Training Results with Employee Performance Management

One of the big trends in learning and development today is the integration of training processes with employee performance management (appraisal and development planning). Ultimately, managers should be measuring the impact of training as part of each employee's annual development and performance management process.

Randstad, for example, uses an LMS platform that includes both learning and performance management (Cornerstone OnDemand). This platform enables line managers to integrate training into the annual development process. Ultimately, training is part of the development and coaching of new employees, so managers and employees own the training process (not the training department). See Figure 5.8 for a sample.

As employees attend training and perform other development assignments, line management assesses them through the performance management process. As the screenshot shown in Figure 5.9 illustrates, managers evaluate employees on their job

Figure 5.8 Integrated Learning and Performance at Randstad

Source: Randstad

Figure 5.9 Performance Assessment Integrated with Learning at Randstad

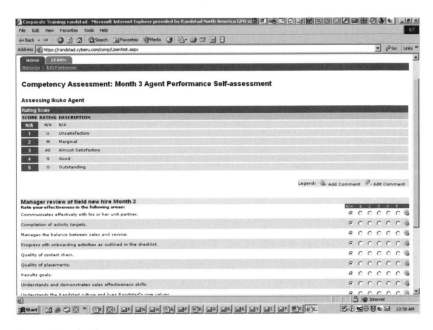

Source: Randstad

performance. The learning and development organization can view this information and use it to determine the effectiveness of their training programs.

More and more LMS systems are starting to implement an integrated solution for both learning and performance management. The goal is to give line managers the authority and responsibility for measuring employees—and evaluating training falls into that role. A training manager can then access this information to help understand the alignment, effectiveness, and impact of the training programs. (This is particularly beneficial when programs are aligned with competencies that are assessed in the performance management process.)

How to Start

As this chapter shows, there are many ways to capture measurement information. Take your time. Every organization that develops a robust and complete measurement program does so over a period of years. HP developed its program over a span of more than five years, and the process continues to evolve.

Initially, you should keep the process simple. The basic steps organizations use are as follows.

Step 1: Establish the Measurement Goals

First, decide what actionable information should be obtained from the measurement program. What decisions do you want to be able to make? Is efficiency an important measure at this point? Is alignment a problem to address?

Review the Impact Model and see which parts of your program lifecycle require the most monitoring and improvement. Look to the problems that need to be solved, and gain agreement on these. For example, is your goal to measure total completion volumes? To measure satisfaction? To give line managers feedback on utility? To understand how well the e-learning programs are being adopted? To understand development productivity? To save money? While each program will have slightly different measurement goals, your first step is to identify the "reasons" for measurement.

Step 2: Review the Impact Framework and Select Key Measures

Once these goals are established, you should review the Impact Framework to see which elements of this process apply to your organization. Using the goals established in the prior step, look through the nine measurement areas and identify some of the key measures to be obtained.

For example, if one of the big challenges is cost-justifying the learning budget, focus on efficiency and alignment measures. These two areas will help to ensure that:

- Training costs are moving down the cost-effectiveness curve; and
- Line managers and executives know that the training dollars are well spent.

Step 3: Develop a Business Unit Signoff Form

Develop a business unit signoff form and make it the first stage of the development process. This is a critical step to building alignment with business units and capturing basic business case information. It will facilitate the alignment process and provide business impact data to help prioritize learning programs and investments.

Step 4: Establish a Performance Consulting Process

It is impossible to align with the business or measure impact without some process for needs analysis or performance consulting. As described earlier in this book, this process will provide the metrics for more detailed impact analysis and establish business goals for each program. The root-cause analysis and business goals can then be used later for impact or utility analysis.

In a relatively small training organization (a few people, perhaps), make sure to have a well-designed "needs analysis" step included in the design process. Among the many books and programs that help organizations implement performance consulting are *Performance Consulting: Moving Beyond Training*[2] and the ASTD Performance Consulting certificate program.

You do not need to reorganize your entire training function to do this, but rather just think about where this process is taking place (I guarantee that someone is doing it). Then look at where you can monitor or measure the inputs and outputs from this process. Is there a "needs analysis" form you can use? Can you document the business requirements for each program on a spreadsheet when you review program status? Can you try to match these requirements against the business unit's key strategic goals? These simple steps will not only improve your alignment, but show you when programs drift out of alignment.

Step 5: Develop a Standard End-of-Course Evaluation

Now for the most important step. Using the guidelines in this report, develop a standard end-of-course evaluation. The HP case study (see Appendix II: Case Study B: HP Develops an Integrated Measurement Process) gives an excellent example of a complete process for building such an evaluation.

What's most important is to keep the evaluation simple and focus on the areas in the Learning Impact Measurement Framework that seem most appropriate to the organization. At a bare minimum, consider all the measurement areas in the Kirkpatrick and Bersin models, and build from there. Remember to capture information that will be considered important and actionable to the organization. The learning and development strategy may drive certain measures, which should be captured here—and sometimes these are unique. In a large pharmaceutical company, for example, all L&D programs must drive some improvement in operational efficiency. Some indicator of the learners' improvement in operational efficiency should be included in their assessments.

A Few Tips to Building Effective Evaluations

Since evaluations and surveys are such an important part of this process, we would like to share some of the best practices identified in the development of these tools.

1. Consistency Is Important. Although it is tempting to customize the evaluation for each course or session, doing so makes analysis far more difficult. Every evaluation should have a basic set of common questions that are asked consistently from program to program. These are the measures that can be compared from program to program, audience to audience, session to session, and year to year. Separate from these would be program-specific questions, which may be created by the performance consultant or instructional designer.

The decision may be to have two-part course evaluations—the "standard" consistent set of questions and a few "program-specific" questions, which may form more of a learning assessment. These latter questions will help the program designer understand how well the learners accomplished their learning objectives and how well the program elements worked for the learners.

2. Capture Indicators, Not Measures. A valuable piece of insight we have learned from the research (and our own survey experience) is the value of measuring indicators. An "indicator" is an individual's assessment of a business outcome, rather than the outcome itself. Although it may be difficult or impossible to capture a real business measure (for example, sales increase), it is very easy to capture an indicator of that measure. The indicators should align with one or more of the Learning Impact Measurement Framework categories.

The following is an example of an indicator that illustrates program utility or business impact. Ask a learner:

How much did this course improve your efficiency at a certain task?

(A) 30 percent or more;

(B) 15 to 30 percent;

(C) 0 to 15 percent; or

(D) Not at all.

Although the answer will not be exactly correct, the indicators received from many learners will be extremely close to the truth and very actionable.

Indicator questions can be created for any type of measure. The important elements of an indicator question are as follows:

• The question should be specific enough that the learner can apply it to his or her particular situation (for instance, "How much did this course help the company improve profits?" is NOT a good question).

- The answer should have a numeric range, forcing the learner to try to quantify the result.

These questions will offer a surrogate for real business metrics. Our experience using this approach with thousands of surveys shows that the answers will be reliable, actionable, and widely varying. They will give excellent information for analysis and, coupled with qualitative comments, such questions can be used for any of the different measure types.

Sample Indicator Questions That Can Be Applied to Any Program.

- How much more efficient do you believe you are in performing your job after taking this course?
- What percent improvement in your work performance do you believe is attributable to this course alone?
- How valuable do you think this course would be to others in your organization?
- How strongly would you recommend this course to others in your role or assignment?

There are many such questions. One of the companies that has mastered this approach is KnowledgeAdvisors. KnowledgeAdvisors sells a complete survey and analysis solution, which includes a large set of ready-made indicators for end-of-course and manager evaluations. Samples are shown in Figures 5.10 and 5.11.

Analysis of Learning Indicators. Figure 5.12, which comes from the KnowledgeAdvisors Metrics That Matter® system, shows some aggregated analysis from learning indicators. As shown, if these questions are asked regularly, there will be very consistent patterns with outliers, which give cause to act.

Figure 5.10 Sample End-of-Course Evaluation Questions

KnowledgeAdvisors

Please help us improve the training program by responding to our brief survey below.

INSTRUCTOR

	Strongly Agree	Strongly Disagree
	7 6 5 4 3 2 1 n/a	
1. The instructor was knowledgeable about the subject.	○ ○ ○ ○ ○ ○ ○ ○	
2. The instructor was prepared and organized for the class.	7 6 5 4 3 2 1 n/a ○ ○ ○ ○ ○ ○ ○ ○	
3. Participants were encouraged to take part in class discussions.	7 6 5 4 3 2 1 n/a ○ ○ ○ ○ ○ ○ ○ ○	
4. The instructor was responsive to participants' needs and questions.	7 6 5 4 3 2 1 n/a ○ ○ ○ ○ ○ ○ ○ ○	
5. The instructor's energy and enthusiasm kept the participants actively engaged.	7 6 5 4 3 2 1 n/a ○ ○ ○ ○ ○ ○ ○ ○	
6. On-the-job application of each objective was discussed during the course.	7 6 5 4 3 2 1 n/a ○ ○ ○ ○ ○ ○ ○ ○	

ENVIRONMENT

	Strongly Agree	Strongly Disagree
	7 6 5 4 3 2 1 n/a	
7. The physical environment was conducive to learning.	○ ○ ○ ○ ○ ○ ○ ○	

COURSEWARE

	Strongly Agree	Strongly Disagree
	7 6 5 4 3 2 1 n/a	
8. The scope of the material was appropriate to meet my needs.	○ ○ ○ ○ ○ ○ ○ ○	
9. The material was organized logically.	7 6 5 4 3 2 1 n/a ○ ○ ○ ○ ○ ○ ○ ○	
10. The examples presented helped me understand the content.	7 6 5 4 3 2 1 n/a ○ ○ ○ ○ ○ ○ ○ ○	
11. The participant materials (manual, presentation handouts, etc.) will be useful on the job.	7 6 5 4 3 2 1 n/a ○ ○ ○ ○ ○ ○ ○ ○	

LEARNING EFFECTIVENESS

	Strongly Agree	Strongly Disagree
	7 6 5 4 3 2 1 n/a	
12. I have learned new knowledge/skills from this training.	○ ○ ○ ○ ○ ○ ○ ○	

13. Rate your **INCREASE** in skill level or knowledge of this content before versus after the training. A 0% is no increase and a 100% is a very significant increase.
□ 0% □ 10% □ 20% □ 30% □ 40% □ 50% □ 60% □ 70% □ 80% □ 90% □ 100%

JOB IMPACT

	Strongly Agree	Strongly Disagree
	7 6 5 4 3 2 1 n/a	
14. I will be able to apply the knowledge and skills learned in this class to my job.	○ ○ ○ ○ ○ ○ ○ ○	

15. What percent of your total work time requires the knowledge and skills presented in this training? Check only one.
□ 0% □ 10% □ 20% □ 30% □ 40% □ 50% □ 60% □ 70% □ 80% □ 90% □ 100%

16. On a scale of **0%** (not at all) to **100%** (extremely critical), how critical is applying the content of this training to your job success? Check one.
□ 0% □ 10% □ 20% □ 30% □ 40% □ 50% □ 60% □ 70% □ 80% □ 90% □ 100%

JOB IMPACT (Continued)

17. What percent of new knowledge and skills learned from this training do you estimate you will directly apply to your job? Check only one.
□ 0% □ 10% □ 20% □ 30% □ 40% □ 50% □ 60% □ 70% □ 80% □ 90% □ 100%

BUSINESS RESULTS

	Strongly Agree	Strongly Disagree
	7 6 5 4 3 2 1 n/a	
18. This training will improve my job performance and productivity.	○ ○ ○ ○ ○ ○ ○ ○	

19. This training will have a significant impact on: (check all that apply)
□ increasing quality □ increasing productivity □ increasing employee satisfaction
□ decreasing costs □ increasing sales □ increasing customer satisfaction
□ decreasing cycle time

For each of the business results you selected in the previous question, please answer the group of questions that pertain to the result(s) you selected.

BUSINESS RESULTS; QUALITY

If you selected **Quality** as a business result, please answer the following questions.

	Strongly Agree	Strongly Disagree
	7 6 5 4 3 2 1 n/a	
20. This training will help me increase quality.	○ ○ ○ ○ ○ ○ ○ ○	

21. Given all factors, including this training, estimate how much quality will increase.
□ 0% □ 5% □ 10% □ 15% □ 20% □ 25% □ 30% □ 35% □ 40% □ 45% □ 50% □ 55% □ 60% □ 65% □ 70% □ 75% □ 80% □ 8%5 □ 90% □ 95% □ 100%

22. Based on your response to the prior question, estimate how much of the improvement will be a direct result of this training. (for example if you feel that half of your improvement is a direct result of the training, enter 50% here.)
□ 0% □ 5% □ 10% □ 15% □ 20% □ 25% □ 30% □ 35% □ 40% □ 45% □ 50% □ 55% □ 60% □ 65% □ 70% □ 75% □ 80% □ 8%5 □ 90% □ 95% □ 100%

BUSINESS RESULTS; PRODUCTIVITY

If you selected **Productivity** as a business result, please answer the following questions.

	Strongly Agree	Strongly Disagree
	7 6 5 4 3 2 1 n/a	
23. This training will help me increase productivity.	○ ○ ○ ○ ○ ○ ○ ○	

24. Given all factors, including this training, estimate how much productivity will increase.
□ 0% □ 5% □ 10% □ 15% □ 20% □ 25% □ 30% □ 35% □ 40% □ 45% □ 50% □ 55% □ 60% □ 65% □ 70% □ 75% □ 80% □ 8%5 □ 90% □ 95% □ 100%

25. Based on your response to the prior question, estimate how much of the improvement will be a direct result of this training. (for example if you feel that half of your improvement is a direct result of the training, enter 50% here.)
□ 0% □ 5% □ 10% □ 15% □ 20% □ 25% □ 30% □ 35% □ 40% □ 45% □ 50% □ 55% □ 60% □ 65% □ 70% □ 75% □ 80% □ 8%5 □ 90% □ 95% □ 100%

Source: KnowledgeAdvisors

Figure 5.11 Sample Follow-Up Questions

BUSINESS RESULTS; EMPLOYEE SATISFACTION

If you selected **Employee Satisfaction** as a business result, please answer the following questions.

Strongly Agree   Strongly Disagree
7 6 5 4 3 2 1 n/a

26. This training will help me increase employee satisfaction. ○ ○ ○ ○ ○ ○ ○ ○

27. Given all factors, including this training, estimate how much employee satisfaction will increase.
☐0% ☐5% ☐10% ☐15% ☐20% ☐25% ☐30% ☐35% ☐40% ☐45% ☐50%
☐55% ☐60% ☐65% ☐70% ☐75% ☐80% ☐85% ☐90% ☐95% ☐100%

28. Based on your response to the prior question, estimate how much of the improvement will be a direct result of this training. (for example if you feel that half of your improvement is a direct result of the training, enter 50% here.)
☐0% ☐5% ☐10% ☐15% ☐20% ☐25% ☐30% ☐35% ☐40% ☐45% ☐50%
☐55% ☐60% ☐65% ☐70% ☐75% ☐80% ☐8% ☐90% ☐95% ☐100%

BUSINESS RESULTS; DECREASING COSTS

If you selected **Decreasing Costs** as a business result, please answer the following questions.

Strongly Agree   Strongly Disagree
7 6 5 4 3 2 1 n/a

29. This training will help me decrease costs. ○ ○ ○ ○ ○ ○ ○ ○

30. Given all factors, including this training, estimate how much costs will decrease.
☐0% ☐5% ☐10% ☐15% ☐20% ☐25% ☐30% ☐35% ☐40% ☐45% ☐50%
☐55% ☐60% ☐65% ☐70% ☐75% ☐80% ☐85% ☐90% ☐95% ☐100%

31. Based on your response to the prior question, estimate how much of the improvement will be a direct result of this training. (for example if you feel that half of your improvement is a direct result of the training, enter 50% here.)
☐0% ☐5% ☐10% ☐15% ☐20% ☐25% ☐30% ☐35% ☐40% ☐45% ☐50%
☐55% ☐60% ☐65% ☐70% ☐75% ☐80% ☐8% ☐90% ☐95% ☐100%

BUSINESS RESULTS; INCREASING SALES

If you selected **Increasing Sales** as a business result, please answer the following questions.

Strongly Agree   Strongly Disagree
7 6 5 4 3 2 1 n/a

32. This training will help me increase sales. ○ ○ ○ ○ ○ ○ ○ ○

33. Given all factors, including this training, estimate how much sales will increase.
☐0% ☐5% ☐10% ☐15% ☐20% ☐25% ☐30% ☐35% ☐40% ☐45% ☐50%
☐55% ☐60% ☐65% ☐70% ☐75% ☐80% ☐85% ☐90% ☐95% ☐100%

34. Based on your response to the prior question, estimate how much of the improvement will be a direct result of this training. (for example if you feel that half of your improvement is a direct result of the training, enter 50% here.)
☐0% ☐5% ☐10% ☐15% ☐20% ☐25% ☐30% ☐35% ☐40% ☐45% ☐50%
☐55% ☐60% ☐65% ☐70% ☐75% ☐80% ☐8% ☐90% ☐95% ☐100%

BUSINESS RESULTS; INCREASING CUSTOMER SATISFACTION

If you selected **Increasing Customer Satisfaction** as a business result, please answer the following questions.

Strongly Agree   Strongly Disagree
7 6 5 4 3 2 1 n/a

35. This training will help me increase customer satisfaction. ○ ○ ○ ○ ○ ○ ○ ○

36. Given all factors, including this training, estimate how much customer satisfaction will increase.
☐0% ☐5% ☐10% ☐15% ☐20% ☐25% ☐30% ☐35% ☐40% ☐45% ☐50%
☐55% ☐60% ☐65% ☐70% ☐75% ☐80% ☐85% ☐90% ☐95% ☐100%

37. Based on your response to the prior question, estimate how much of the improvement will be a direct result of this training. (for example if you feel that half of your improvement is a direct result of the training, enter 50% here.)
☐0% ☐5% ☐10% ☐15% ☐20% ☐25% ☐30% ☐35% ☐40% ☐45% ☐50%
☐55% ☐60% ☐65% ☐70% ☐75% ☐80% ☐85 ☐90% ☐95% ☐100%

BUSINESS RESULTS; DECREASING CYCLE TIME

If you selected **Decreasing Cycle Time** as a business result, please answer the following questions.

Strongly Agree   Strongly Disagree
7 6 5 4 3 2 1 n/a

38. This training will help me decrease cycle time. ○ ○ ○ ○ ○ ○ ○ ○

39. Given all factors, including this training, estimate how much cycle time will decrease.
☐0% ☐5% ☐10% ☐15% ☐20% ☐25% ☐30% ☐35% ☐40% ☐45% ☐50%
☐55% ☐60% ☐65% ☐70% ☐75% ☐80% ☐85% ☐90% ☐95% ☐100%

40. Based on your response to the prior question, estimate how much of the improvement will be a direct result of this training. (for example if you feel that half of your improvement is a direct result of the training, enter 50% here.)
☐0% ☐5% ☐10% ☐15% ☐20% ☐25% ☐30% ☐35% ☐40% ☐45% ☐50%
☐55% ☐60% ☐65% ☐70% ☐75% ☐80% ☐8% ☐90% ☐95% ☐100%

RETURN ON INVESTMENT

Strongly Agree   Strongly Disagree
7 6 5 4 3 2 1 n/a

41. This training was a worthwhile investment in my career development. ○ ○ ○ ○ ○ ○ ○ ○

7 6 5 4 3 2 1 n/a

42. This training was a worthwhile investment for my employer. ○ ○ ○ ○ ○ ○ ○ ○

What about this class was **most** useful to you?

_____

What about this class was **least** useful to you?

_____

How can we improve the training to make it more relevant to your job?

_____

Would you like to be notified about advanced or complementary courses? ○ Yes ○ No

Source: KnowledgeAdvisors

Figure 5.12 Indicator Analysis

End of program performance summary

	1/1 to 3/31	10/1 to 12/31
Respondents in analysis	284,269	269,635
Quality	High	High
Very satisfied with overall program	76.20%	78.60%
Very satisfied with instructor performance	88.10%	88.00%
Very satisfied with content and delivery	67.70%	70.50%
Effectiveness	Very High	Very High
Experienced significant knowledge and skills gains	71.30%	71.80%
Projected Impact	High	High
Definitely plan to apply knowledge/skills on job	66.00%	67.00%
Expect on-the-job performance to improve significantly	57.30%	58.50%
Predicted improvement in performance due to training (adjusted for bias)	7.30%	7.00%
Results	High	High
Expect the program will significantly impact increasing quality	62.20%	61.90%
Expect the program will significantly impact decreasing costs	21.50%	16.50%
Expect the program will significantly impact decreasing cycle time	42.10%	36.30%
Expect the program will significantly impact increasing Productivity	62.60%	65.40%
Expect the program will significantly impact increasing sales	10.80%	9.10%
Expect the program will significantly impact increasing customer satisfaction	40.50%	36.50%
Expect the program will significantly impact increasing employee satisfaction	36.30%	36.30%
Value	High	High
Felt program was a very worthwhile investment	69.30%	69.70%
Projected benefit to cost ration from training	3.5 to 1	3.5 to 1

Source: KnowledgeAdvisors

Notes

1. For more information, see The High-Impact Learning Organization: WhatWorks® in *The Management, Organization, and Governance of Corporate Training*. Bersin & Associates, June 2005. Available at www.bersin.com.
2. Robinson, D.G., & Robinson, J.C. (1995). *Performance Consulting: Moving Beyond Training*. San Francisco, CA: Berrett-Koehler.

Chapter Six

Measurement of Business Impact

One of the most daunting challenges in corporate training is the measurement of true business impact. Since training is a "soft" expenditure item, organizations are constantly trying to answer the question: "What business benefits are we achieving from this expense?"

Before discussing best practices and approaches to the measurement of impact, let me discuss the whole concept first.

In general, as this book describes throughout, I find a bit too much energy and worry focused in this area. Remember the principles of training measurement we discussed earlier: Is the information credible, specific, and actionable? When one tries to measure direct business impact, the results rarely fit these criteria, because, as we all know, for every business measure, there are usually many factors that have far more impact than training.

In most cases the reason an organization attempts to measure direct business impact is because they are not well aligned, the program is too expensive, or the training is not well regarded. Hence they try to use impact measures to try to "cost-justify" their programs.

One CLO I regard very highly told me he puts it this way.

"I ask my line of business customers if they believe in the value of workforce learning and development as part of their business strategy. If they say yes, then I know my measurements should focus on alignment and utility. If they say no, then I know that no amount of ROI or other such measurements will convince them, and I have other problems to solve."

In the meantime, there are many ways to measure the business impact of training with the goal of not "cost-justifying training" but, rather, better understanding precisely how programs work and how they can be improved or, perhaps, even eliminated.

Of course, despite these challenges, we still want to know how our training programs drive value—because ultimately this will give us actionable information about how to make them better. So how can we use the principles discussed earlier to most effectively measure impact?

Simplifying the Problem

Let us go back to the Impact Measurement Framework and reorient it using two dimensions. In Figure 6.1, all possible measures of training are organized on two axes: those which are

Figure 6.1 Measuring Impact: The Options

Where does it fit?

	Qualitative	Quantitative
Business measures	Alignment and attainment individual and organizational performance "Did you see results?" "How much?" Indicators not measures	Hardest to measure Requires sales or production data hard to isolate training effect 1. Line-of-business-specific 2. Performance management centric
Training measures	Satisfaction, learning "Was this worth your time?" Indicators and End-of-course surveys	Efficiency and adoption Enrollment rates Completion rates Satisfaction levels Scores Total hours

qualitative versus quantitative on the vertical axis, and those which are truly business measures (for example, sales and customer satisfaction) and those which are training measures (for example, learner satisfaction and scores) on the horizontal axis.

Now try to locate each of the nine measures from Learning Impact Measurement Framework on this chart. Most can be placed in the shaded boxes, which use the techniques discussed in this book: indicators of impact through surveys, interviews, scores, and other more qualitative approaches.

So how do all these measures directly correlate to business results? As shown in the upper-right quadrant of Figure 6.1, we have found essentially two easy, repeatable approaches: line-of-business-specific measures and performance management measures.

Use Line-of-Business-Specific Measures

In every organization, there are already a large number of business measurements already being recorded. Sales managers are measuring sales productivity and revenue. Call center managers are measuring call times, customer satisfaction, and sales volume per call. Hospitals are measuring patient satisfaction, patient outcomes, errors, skin conditions, falls, and many other operational errors. Financial services companies are measuring loan processing errors, customer loyalty, and so on. These measures are part of the organization's "balanced scorecard" or general management processes.

During the performance consulting process (again we reinforce why this is so important), which starts with the business unit signoff form, the program manager should identify which of these existing metrics represents an important measure of the problem. These "line-of-business measures" are usually not enough to fully diagnose the solution because they measure the "outcome" and not the "cause" of the problem. To drive impact, focus on improvements to these existing measures.

Once these sources of data have been identified, then follow the performance consulting process shown in Figure 6.2 to diagnose the causes of the problem to be solved. These root causes, which can also be measured, will then lead to the right training solution.

If the problem identified is vague (for instance, "We're not selling enough of product A"), then a solution cannot be prescribed. It must be broken down to its cause (for example, "Our sales reps are not demonstrating the product in enough detail to overcome competitor A's land mines"). Once the root cause (or causes) is identified, it is a simple step to identify some way of quantifying this problem (for instance, "Seventy-five percent of the demonstrations we do should directly cover topics A, B, and C").

Figure 6.2 Performance Consulting Process Drives Problem Identification

Performance consulting function

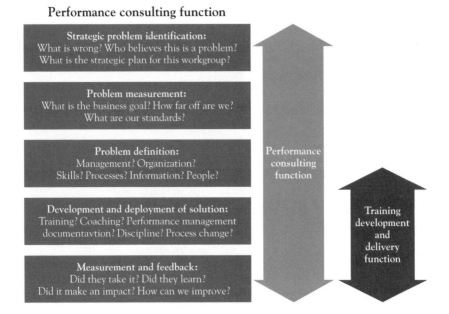

Example: Insurance Call Center Training

A client of ours, a major insurance company, operates a large call center staffed with claims agents. These individuals take calls from customers who file claims. There are many steps to this process: looking up the customer in the system, identifying what coverage they have, taking information and phone recordings describing the claim, collecting supporting documentation and receipts, judging which claim items are covered and which are not, and then settling the claim. Overall, this is a highly complex role that can have a major impact on the profitability of the company.

This particular company measures many aspects of this operation: number of calls, time to take a claim, time to complete a claim, error rates in claim processing, as well as average claim amounts correlated against many demographics. As one can see, some of these metrics capture customer service measures (time to take a claim, time to complete a claim), some capture quality measures (error rates, claim amounts), and some capture profitability (average claim amounts by different agents handling similar customers and similar claims).

The "problem" identified by the customer service department was that "claim processing is too slow," therefore the group needs more training. This particular training department was very savvy, so they saw right through this "problem" and realized that they had to do a much deeper diagnosis of the problem. They implemented some call center monitoring software (from a company called Epiance) that analyzes average time between different steps in the claims process. These steps go on for many weeks and months, so the database collected was very large.

As they started to analyze this data, some interesting facts emerged: some of the agents (about 10 percent) were filing claims at 3 to 4X the speed of others. These "speedy agents" were believed to be the senior, most highly trained experts who best understood the system and process. Most of the agents

144 THE TRAINING MEASUREMENT BOOK

(70 percent) were processing claims at similar rates. And a small number of "slow" agents (20 percent) were processing claims far slower than the average. Now the question was: How do we improve speed? Do we see what the "speedy" agents are doing and try to replicate those skills? Or do we look at what the "slow" agents are doing and try to fix their problems?

Well luckily, this particular training manager was very business-focused. He decided to go one step further, and he also looked at the "audit rates" of different groups. What he found was astounding. The "fast" agents were actually skipping several important steps in the process (such as checking whether or not a claim was covered). They were being rewarded for "speed" but not "quality"—and of course this was costing the company a lot of money. The "slow" agents were actually delivering the highest levels of customer service, and they were paying approximately the same claim amounts as the "average."

The resulting learning programs were then focused on three things: (1) assuring that all agents clearly understood the importance of each and every step in the process; (2) making sure that agents knew how to "speed up" calls through careful interviewing and objection handling; and (3) making sure all agents were familiar with the systems that support each step. They also added an important module about company profitability and how the company's claims processing strategy supported both their customer service and profitability strategy.

Once this was done, it was fairly easy to figure out what to measure. As the program progressed, the team measured these three groups again, measured claim quality and customer service, and looked at whether or not claim amounts were increasing. As this data was collected, the program was "tweaked" to further reinforce process and not systems training. The result, a "training program" that had tremendously high return to the business.

Do you implement a rigorous performance consulting process? Fewer than 40 percent of our respondents claim to have such a process, and under 10 percent consider themselves excellent at this step. I challenge you to implement one *immediately*. It is the single greatest contributor to high-impact learning programs.[1]

How do you implement such a process? Consider the process shown in the following diagram (compliments of a large bank). In this organization, as Figure 6.3 shows, learning consultants are trained to start at the top (business measures) and work their way down to specific skills and knowledge that drive these results.

The training director who sponsors this process told us that he is rarely, if ever, asked to quantify the business value of the training. This process gets them so intimately involved in the business issues at hand that the line managers never question the value or alignment of the training.

Once the program manager or consultant has gone through this diagnosis and identified the existing measures that are impacted, it is easy to then monitor these measures and the related causes to see results.

Example: Pharmaceutical Sales

Consider another example. In one particular pharmaceutical company, the sales organization (more than seven thousand sales representatives) uses a process called "field trip reports" to measure the effectiveness of a sales call. The sales manager goes out with the sales rep for certain calls and fills out an assessment form that grades the sales rep on a variety of measures (for example, ability to create rapport, ability to diagnose the right problem, ability to effectively present the right product, and so on). The field trip reports are then sent to an electronic database, which resides in the sales training organization. The sales training organization can look at these reports and analyze them by sales call type, sales rep, manager, geography, and so on (see Figure 6.4).

The field trip reports follow a standardized format, which identifies the salesperson's success at various skills, competencies, and product-related knowledge in the field. These field

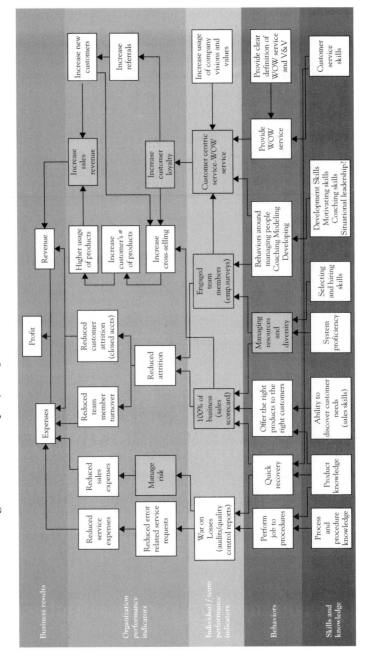

Figure 6.3 A Step-by-Step Process for Performance Consulting

Figure 6.4 Pharmaceutical Sales Measurement Example

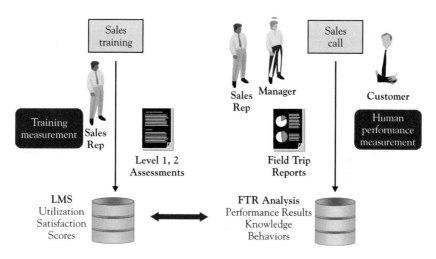

trip reports are, in essence, an indicator of sales volume that has already been categorized. They are a direct measure of "individual performance" in the Bersin model.

For this company, the sales training manager can directly view the results and impact of a new program by monitoring the data in the field trip reports. The sales training manager does not have to guess at other business measures—he or she can build on an existing measure that is well-understood. There is no reason to measure "level 3" or "level 4" data, because it is already being captured in a highly relevant way.

Example: Healthcare Outcome Data

A third example of the use of line-of-business data is in healthcare. One of the interviewees from this research is the CLO of a small chain of hospitals. The most critical part of the training operation is the training of clinical personnel—mostly nurses and other service-delivery staff.

In the hospital and healthcare industry, there are a wide variety of existing measures being captured every day. In this particular case, the hospital tracks falls, needle pricks, infections, skin conditions, and a wide variety of other health-related measures for patients in the hospital. The organization uses a third party (Picker Institute) to measure patient satisfaction. This data can be compared against many other hospitals of similar size and structure.

The CLO uses these two data sources to identify problem areas that must be addressed by clinical training. He or she can see whether trends are good or bad, view data by hospital and by department, and by manager. This data has become so valuable that the CLO no longer needs to use a needs-analysis process to determine where to apply training resources—he or she can "chase the needle" and make sure that the training investments are always aligned and focused on the most critical problems at hand.

When working closely with lines of business in the organization and using a performance consulting process, many of these systems are already in place. The goal should be to use this information, and capture only the data that can be used to measure impact and gain actionable information for improvement.

Bottom line: look for existing business measures during your needs analysis and performance consulting and use them to measure the effectiveness of your programs.

Integrate with Performance Management Processes

A second, fast-growing way to measure and monitor the business impact of training is to monitor and measure the change in manager-driven performance ratings of employees. "Performance management," the term used to describe the process of coaching, goal-setting, appraising, and developing employees, is now a very hot topic in corporate HR.

Most companies have a performance management process[2] that is designed with seven steps: goal development, goal alignment, manager assessment, self-assessment, competency assessment, 360-degree assessment, and development planning. The outcome of this process is typically a performance "rating" (typically a number) and a series of competency assessments. These competency assessments are used to gauge an employee's "potential" for improvement and future roles. The development plan is then designed to fill in these competency gaps and help the employees improve their performance.

How does this relate to training? In many ways. First and foremost, if your organization is using a well-designed performance management process, then managers are regularly assessing employees against goal attainment and competencies. Much of this information is now being automated and put online, through the implementation of automated performance management software. (Most LMS vendors have such software.)

Organizations that have an automated performance management process (or an integrated talent management platform) can actually see the impact of training on performance ratings and view how well learning programs are being correlated to individual and workgroup goals. In fact, if you have access to this system, you can see where development gaps exist, where the most urgent development needs are, and how individual groups and teams are improving before and after training. Best of all, this work is done by the individual line managers—the person who can best evaluate an employee's workplace performance and skills.

Example: Randstad Onboarding Process

One of the detailed case studies included in this book is the case study on Randstad's onboarding program (see Appendix I: Case Study A: Randstad Measures Onboarding). As part of that training program, the Randstad CLO monitors and measures the performance ratings of new hires to make sure they are achieving the skills they need through the onboarding process (see Figure 6.5).

This evaluation is not an evaluation of the training itself but, rather, an evaluation of the employee, which takes place within the performance management process. By tying the training to job-related competencies, this data can be easily captured to truly measure the impact of the L&D programs.

Although many organizations do not yet have an integrated and automated performance and learning management platform, 60 percent or more of companies participating in this research have some type of enterprise performance management process. When spending large sums of money on training that supports particular job roles (for example, management training,

Figure 6.5 Randstad Competency Assessment During Performance Management

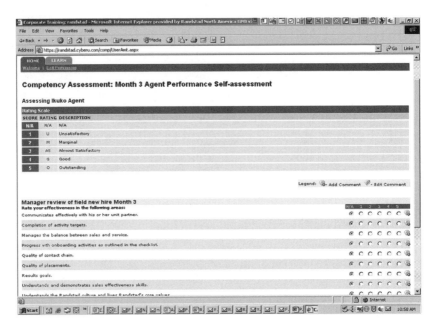

executive education, service center training, or onboarding), seek out this data to better understand and measure the true impact of the training on employee performance, readiness for promotion, and other measures.

Notes

1. For more information, see The High-Impact Learning Organization: WhatWorks® in *The Management, Organization, and Governance of Corporate Training*. Bersin & Associates, June 2005. Available at www.bersin.com.
2. For more information, see High Impact Performance Management®: Comprehensive Industry Study, in *Market Analysis, Trends, Best Practices, and Vendor Profiles*. Bersin & Associates/ Josh Bersin, June 2006. Available at www.bersin.com.

Chapter Seven

Measurement of Alignment

One of the new measures in our Learning Impact Measurement Framework is the measurement of "alignment." Alignment is a critically important topic to training managers. When L&D managers are asked what their biggest challenges are, "being better aligned with the business" continually comes up as one of the top three challenges. We have found that business alignment is one of the most important and challenging areas to focus on.

What does the term "alignment" mean and how can you measure it?

To put it simply, alignment means working on the right programs at the right time. It means that your program investments are focusing on the most important and urgent business problems. It means that management (HR and line-of-business) understands and agrees with the allocation of resources. If the training function is well-aligned, the employees and executives in the organizations can say, "Yes, the training organization is delivering strategic value to our organization."

Why is alignment so difficult? Because training organizations are continuously bombarded with demands for training programs in hundreds of areas across the organization. If you consider the number of different skill areas needed in a five-thousand-person company, the potential areas of investment are staggering: sales, product training, customer service training, technical education, management and leadership training, product training, IT training—the list goes on and on.

Sound business alignment cannot be created without an integrated budgeting, management, and governance process—and measurement is critical to this process. The process should solve the following problems:

- How does a training manager decide where to spend money?
- How does a training manager decide which programs warrant heavy investments and which should be outsourced to low-cost commodity providers?
- Should training focus on the manager who screams the loudest or the business unit with the most money?
- How can the training organization meet rapid demands for new training on products, processes, and services that come along during the year?
- What expectations should business units have for the timeliness, relevance, and investments in different programs?

Our High Impact Learning Organization research[1] finds that there is a set of well-designed best-practice planning and budgeting processes that make this process workable. Many training managers are overwhelmed with the demands for their services. The training manager's job should not be to try to predict or decide where these priorities are but, rather, to implement a planning and governance process that makes sure that line and HR executives participate in the planning process and understand where resources are invested.[2]

For measurement purposes, however, the following examples will explain some best-practice approaches to build and measure alignment.

Caterpillar's Planning and Budgeting Process

Let us examine the example provided by Caterpillar University, a well-established corporate training organization, which supports a wide variety of needs for more than 95,000 employees in nearly two hundred countries. A key to Caterpillar's alignment success is their budgeting and planning process.

At Caterpillar, each business unit creates its own business goals, aligned to the corporate goals. A business unit that manufactures tractors in Japan, for example, must create plans to meet the company's market share, sales, and profit goals for Japan.

In the development of these plans, the business units create individual learning plans for their employees. These divisional learning plans are then "rolled up" into business unit learning plans, which are then shared with Caterpillar University.

As Figure 7.1 shows, each of these divisional learning plans is rolled up by Caterpillar University into a Caterpillar Enterprise Learning Plan. This enterprise plan is the sum total of all individual and business plans, driven by the enterprise's business strategy.

Figure 7.1 Alignment and Business Planning at Caterpillar

Alignment of learning to business goals

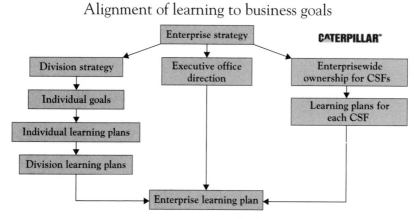

The division learning plan (DLP) is key
• Identify learning required to achieve your strategy
• Plan the learning
• Establish targets and metrics

This is certainly a powerful process if conducted once a year; however, the way it stays aligned is through regular meetings with line-of-business directors to make sure that the learning plans (that is, programs being developed and delivered) are kept up-to-date with changes in the business.

CNA Insurance Training Investment Model

Another example of a powerful and easy-to-use planning and alignment approach is the model developed by CNA Insurance—its "learning investment portfolio." In this model, all training programs are mapped against four quadrants, as shown in Figure 7.2.

The horizontal axis indicates the "strategic nature" of the program: Is it an operational program to "run the business," which drives cost-reduction or productivity (to the left)? Or is it a highly strategic program to "advance the strategy," which

Figure 7.2 CNA Learning Investment Portfolio

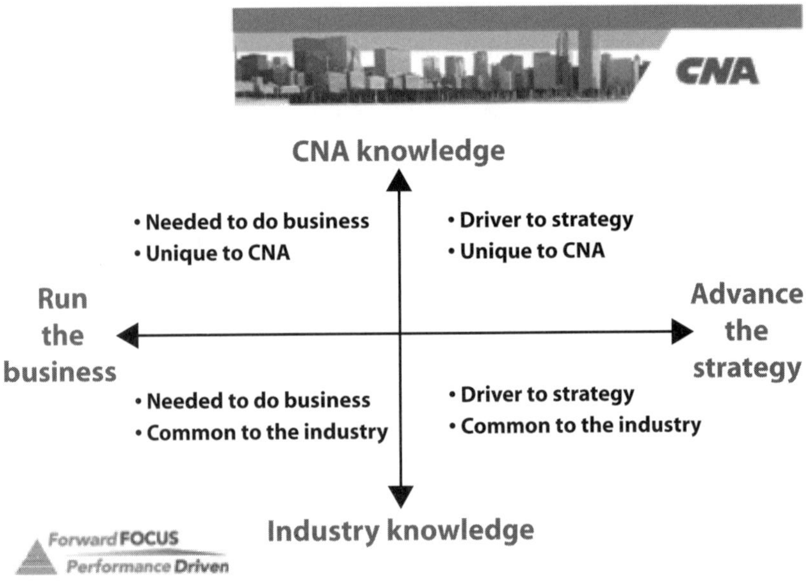

drives competitive advantage (to the right)? The vertical axis indicates whether the program is available "off the shelf" (bottom) or whether it is unique to CNA (top).

CNA works with line managers to take each individual training program and map it to these four quadrants. Lower-left quadrant programs are "commodity" in nature—they are outsourced to e-learning or other external providers. Lower-right programs are more highly funded, but still outsourced to third parties for development. Upper-left programs are built internally, and are funded to meet operational and business planning demands. Upper-right programs are highly funded to drive strategic new initiatives.

To make this process rigorous, CNA makes fixed investment decisions that target that 40 percent of all funding goes to the upper right, 20 percent to the upper left, 30 percent to the lower right, and 10 percent to the bottom left (these numbers are only illustrative). The key to this model is how the map is built: CNA creates this portfolio map through a series of planning meetings with business managers so that each manager can see the relative priorities of his or her needs against the overall organization.[3] Figure 7.3 shows an example of such an investment allocation.

Again, the key to this model is engagement by line-of-business managers on a continual basis, so that decisions can be made in an open manner. It also allows everyone in the organization to see the tradeoffs L&D must make to keep its budget under control.

How Do You Measure Alignment?

Assuming you implement such a planning process, how can you then measure alignment over time? How can you institutionalize and monitor it? Here you have many easy-to-implement options.

Figure 7.3 CNA Sample Program Investment Allocation

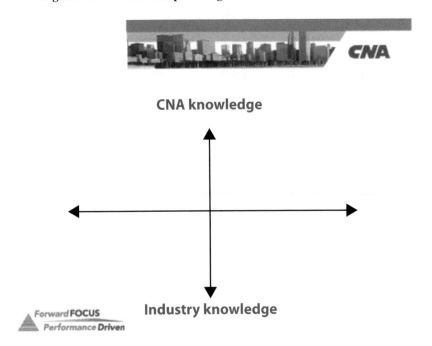

CNA knowledge

Industry knowledge

Measure Alignment of the Overall Learning Organization

To build and measure overall alignment, you must have an established governance process. The term "governance" refers to the processes you use to set priorities and make ongoing decisions.

Typically our best-practice research indicates the organizations need three levels of committees to establish governance:

1. An executive steering committee that sets annual budgets and long-term strategy and approves large capital investments;

2. A series of "learning councils," with representation by both L&D and line-of-business representatives, which reviews plans monthly or quarterly (these are often organized by discipline or business unit); and

3. A number of internal staff meetings within the training organization that serve to manage ongoing operations.

The key to making this work is a written learning business plan. Our research shows that fewer than 50 percent of training organizations have such a plan. If you have such a plan, it should establish goals for program volumes, strategic investments, and key program areas.

The steering committee should review progress against the annual plan and budget. It should meet regularly and have executive-level sponsorship (VP of HR or higher). At Textron, for example, the Executive Council includes the senior vice president of strategy and planning.

All new programs and major changes should require line-of-business signoff, through the signoff form. These approved programs should be monitored regularly, and measures such as adoption, utility, satisfaction, and compliance should be reviewed at each meeting of the appropriate learning council. The purpose of the learning council is not only to "report on progress" but also to enlist help. If a certain program is failing (for instance, low attendance), it is in the interest of the business unit managers to help it succeed. Each program should have its executive sponsor also listed, so that representatives can go back to this sponsor if higher-level communication is needed.

Organizational alignment requires all these steps. And the measurement process should consist of a dashboard of measures for each program, organized by business unit, that shows the business unit managers the health and status of each training program. Some organizations include a checklist for each program to monitor its progress through the check-off process. Others implement lists of programs that are going through various stages of signoff and their stated business benefits ("potential ROI"). You can easily implement such a process as part of your quarterly or monthly program review meetings. Some excellent examples of organization alignment reports are shown in the

Defense Acquisition University screenshots. (See Appendix IV: Examples of Learning Measurements).

Measuring Alignment of Individual Programs

On a program-by-program level, alignment measures should track how well the training organization is communicating with and listening to line managers. You should create a spreadsheet of the impact measures you have decided to track, such as adoption rate, ongoing satisfaction and utility measures, and learning results (if measured). Each line of this report should also include the program name, its "potential ROI," and sponsor.

You can also track the performance consulting for each program by including a short phrase or paragraph in the report that summarizes the key root problems this program is attempting to solve.

If manager assessments are being used, they can also be tracked in this dashboard. How well does the manager rate the value of this program against the time invested by his or her employees? (This is a "utility" or "alignment" measure that can be captured through a manager survey or interviews.) How well do learners rate their managers' support for their attendance and application of the skills obtained in this program? (This is an "alignment" measure that can be captured through an end-of-course survey.)

Manager alignment is a measure you should strongly consider. Here is an example of a major program that suffered from lack of management alignment:

In one division of KPMG, for example, many of the training programs are developed and delivered by a national training organization. This organization surveys the regional accounting and consulting teams, creates programs to meet perceived demand, and then launches and manages these programs. Individual consultants take these programs and often rate them very highly.

Because the training organization is separate from each geographic and industry unit, they have to balance needs for professional development with specific industry and certification requirements.

The CLO reviews satisfaction surveys for each course and finds that most programs are rated highly. However, when the CLO started to ask employees how well programs were supported by their line-of-business managers, the ratings were fairly low. Many programs were not supported by line management.

Why was this? The CLO believes that line managers are not familiar enough with the learning offerings and that the company is letting employees "self-select" what learning they take. Although this can be highly valuable in building a self-learning organization, it is a sign of poor alignment. Either line managers do not understand or do not appreciate the value of the learning programs, or perhaps the L&D organization is not focusing on the most urgent business problems. This is a perfect example of where the Kirkpatrick model breaks down. The training may, in fact, improve job performance; however, the programs being delivered may not be focusing on the most important areas of performance to the line organization.

There are many potential solutions to this problem: alignment with performance planning, a more integrated planning process, or reorganizing the learning organization into line-of-business support teams.

Using indicators and qualitative interviews with line managers, training organizations can create their own scorecards of alignment. A manager or learner indicator, such as "How strategic was this training program to your most current and urgent business needs?" is a perfect way of measuring alignment.

I recently asked the CLO of a major telecommunications equipment provider how she measured the business alignment of each program. She had a simple answer: "I ask my learning managers to tell me the most strategic problems in their customer organizations. I then compare these notes to the information I hear from these customers themselves. If they match, we're fine—if they don't, I know I have a problem."

Sophisticated organizations, such as the Defense Acquisition University (DAU), regularly poll their business executive customers to ask such questions. Sometimes a program is urgent but not strategic (for instance, a mandatory compliance program); at other times, a program is strategic but not urgent (for instance, CNA's underwriting training program). The only way to make sure the alignment is in place is by continually measuring alignment and developing a process for regularly validating priorities with business managers.

Notes

1. For more information, see The High-Impact Learning Organization: WhatWorks® in *The Management, Organization, and Governance of Corporate Training*. Bersin & Associates, June 2005 and new release coming in 2008. Available at www.bersin.com.
2. Ibid. Also available are High-Impact Learning Organization workshops at www.bersin.com.
3. For more information, see *The Training Investment Model: How to Allocate Training Investments for Optimum Business Impact*. Bersin & Associates, February 2005. Available at www.bersin.com.

Chapter Eight

Attainment: Measurement of Customer Satisfaction

One of the new measurement areas we specify in the Learning Impact Measurement Framework is "attainment," which refers to the measurement of how well the organization has met specific customer requirements. This could be considered the "customer satisfaction" measure. This measure, not considered in the Kirkpatrick model, may be the most important one of all.

Remember that Learning & Development is a service organization and, as such, customer satisfaction should be your *number-one goal*. In the service business, customer satisfaction measures are defined by the *customer*—not by you. Customers establish the criteria for success. Some program sponsors may measure success by being delivered on-time, for example. Others may measure success by being delivered on-budget. Others may measure success by meeting their limited time requirements, technology requirements, or learner satisfaction requirements.

This measure, called "voice of the customer" in Six Sigma terms, is one of the most valuable measurement processes used in manufacturing, sales, and other business processes. It should be incorporated into the measurement program. Let me briefly introduce you to some Six Sigma concepts.

The Six Sigma Approach

Six Sigma[1] is an approach for measuring, monitoring, and improving manufacturing and business processes to generate the highest possible quality results. It was developed with the goal of establishing a clear process to measure and improve the quality of any business process. It has been refined through implementation at hundreds of companies, and elements of it can easily be applied to training. The Depository Trust Clearing Corporation (DTCC) uses Six Sigma to measure training development, delivery, and customer satisfaction.

Simply explained, Six Sigma lays out a set of processes to define:

- Customer needs and measures of success
- Customer "critical-to-quality" issues (the things that "must be done right" in order for the customer to be successful)
- Processes that result in this quality (processes in your training organization, in the rollout, delivery, or follow-up)
- Measures of the performance of these processes (indicators of each process, such as those in the Impact Measurement Framework®)
- A way to collect and analyze this data
- A commitment to continually use this data to improve these processes through solutions (process improvement, training, etc.)
- Ongoing improvements over time

Six Sigma is a process that goes on forever. You establish these measures and you monitor them at all times, continually making process improvements and increasing your measures to get better and better over time. Six Sigma enables Japanese auto manufacturers to develop higher and higher quality automobiles every year. When a new car is designed (as when a new learning program is designed), the measures and processes must be applied to this new car. Processes that were highly successful in a prior car (or learning program) may need tweaking or improvement in a new car (or program).

For example, suppose one of your Six Sigma measures is the ability to deliver a program precisely on-time. This may be customer-critical for a product launch. If you are ten days late on an original schedule of one hundred days of development, this would represent a 10 percent schedule slip. For a subsequent program, you may be five days behind on a development schedule of twenty weeks, or 2.5 percent schedule slip. To meet the "Six Sigma" goals, you would strive to be 100 percent on-time more than 99.9 percent of the time (a very lofty goal).

In Six Sigma terminology, the success of an improvement is measured by how well the training organization meets the customers' critical-to-quality issues—*as defined by the customer.*

In Six Sigma, these criteria are specific and unique to each customer. For example, for a compliance program, the customer may have a requirement that 100 percent of employees successfully complete the program by a certain date. There may not be any learning or business objectives beyond this. Here, success may be measured by completion rate. In a food-safety program, the customer's criteria of success may be a 90 percent or higher score on the exit exam. This is a "learning" objective.

A training organization should capture these requirements on the signoff form (or during the performance consulting process) and establish a process for capturing this data to meet the customer's needs. Can success be gauged against these customer-driven requirements? Yes.

How Close Is the Training Organization to Perfection?

Six Sigma addresses this question. The term "sigma" refers to the statistical standard deviation (a measure of how much variance there is in the results). In a sense, the sigma level is "how close we are to perfection."

In Six Sigma terms, perfection is defined by these customer requirements. A Six Sigma *defect* is defined as anything outside of these customer specifications.

Suppose, again, that one customer's issue is "time to market"—the customer needs the course to be out in three weeks. If 90 percent of the time the course is delivered within three weeks, then the training organization is between 4 Sigma and 5 Sigma. A second customer requirement may be cost. The client demands that the program come in on-budget. If the ability to meet this need is measured and it is achieved 66 percent of the time, only 2 Sigma has been attained (far below 6).

How Do You Operationalize the Measurement of Customer Satisfaction?

Once you come to grips with the "attainment" of "customer satisfaction" concept, it is not difficult to measure. At DTCC Learning, the Six Sigma approach is used to measure every single learning program. The voice-of-the-customer requirements are identified up-front, turned into specifications, and then used to measure the sigma of each measure and, ultimately, the program itself. Programs can then be ranked by their "sigma" results.

For example, if one of the Six Sigma measures was on-time delivery, DTCC measures the "days behind schedule" for each program. If another measure was meeting budget compliance, it is easy to measure the "percent over budget" for each program. If a third measure is "percent of target audience completed within 180 days," then again this can easily be measured.

Note that "How satisfied was the customer?" is not a Kirkpatrick measure, so if you follow the traditional Kirkpatrick model you may miss it completely.

We encourage every training organization to capture these voice-of-the-customer needs through a business unit signoff form or performance consulting process. These processes can then track progress against goals and use these as a way of "scoring" delivery success. You can establish a set of eight to ten of these measures yourself and easily develop your own benchmarks.

These benchmark measures serve two important values: first, they will give you excellent operational targets to improve your learning operations; second, they will give your business unit customers tremendous confidence in your organization.

Notes

1. For more information on Six Sigma, please visit www.sixsigma. com, which offers articles and easy-to-read examples of how to apply Six Sigma to any business process.

Chapter Nine

Measurement Tools and Technologies

Ultimately, whatever measures you decide to capture, you will be forced to collect a lot of data from a lot of people. There have been many products and technologies developed to help companies implement a training measurement program. While this book is not intended to be a detailed discussion of Learning Management Systems (LMS)[1] and analytics systems,[2] here we highlight some of the important tools and technologies to consider.

The Role of the LMS

Let me again emphasize how important it is to use your LMS. One of the most important issues in training measurement is capturing and storing the data in one single place—the LMS should be this place. By its very design, the LMS will capture adoption data and compliance data and also hold all the detailed demographic and job-related information about learners. If you use the LMS for data capture, you can then easily correlate and aggregate data. (This is further explained in Appendix VI of this book.)

When we asked organizations about the effectiveness of their LMS in measurement, the results were fairly low. Only 10 percent of the respondents to our 2006 survey rated the LMS excellent in reporting, and only 29 percent excellent or high, as shown in Figure 9.1.

Figure 9.1 Ability of LMS to Deliver Measurement and Reporting

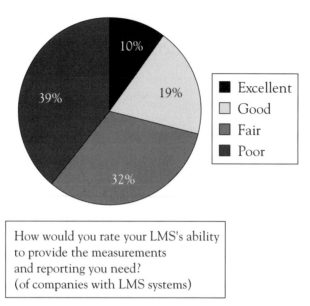

How would you rate your LMS's ability
to provide the measurements
and reporting you need?
(of companies with LMS systems)

Data Integration and Standards

There are several reasons for these ratings. First, if you have not developed a measurement program, the LMS is not likely to have all the information you need. You have to make sure that assessment, tracking, survey, and other information is captured in the form you desire. Since so few companies have well-developed measurement programs, they cannot simply "hope" that their LMS will give them all the information they need.

Second, in order for information to be highly actionable, the LMS must contain accurate information about all the dimensions of training: employees, programs, customers, and all their surrounding characteristics. This requires data from other systems (for example, HRMS, CRM, and others) that is current and accurate. Finally, as we discussed earlier in this book, data in the LMS should adhere to standards. For example:

- Does your organization have a naming standard for courses, sessions, events, webcasts, and related learning objects?
- Does your organization test all e-learning programs to make sure they capture and store the right tracking and completion data?
- Does your organization regularly update employee information to include current job level, manager, and other demographic data?
- How does the training function handle temporary employees or part-time workers?
- How does the organization handle customers, resellers, and channel partners?

These data integration challenges are not trivial. They often make up 20 to 30 percent of the total investment in implementation, management, and maintenance of the LMS system. In most organizations, the biggest benefit to an LMS system is its role as the "single system of record" for training. Yet most organizations have not made the investment in the integration, standards, and processes to make sure this data is current and accurate. We strongly urge organizations to take this problem seriously—without accurate data, it is nearly impossible to effectively manage the large L&D investment.

Our market research finds that, on average, organizations spend between 0 and 5 percent of their overall training budget on measurement, with an average of 2.4 percent. Organizations that rate their measurement processes high tend to spend almost 50 percent more on training measurement than those that rate their measurement processes as low. I think a sound and reasonable number to target is 3 percent. Part of this budget should go into standards and processes to make sure that data captured in the LMS is consistent.

Reporting and Analytics Tools

The other challenge organizations have with their LMSs is the difficulty to create easy-to-understand reports from the system itself. In our LMS customer satisfaction research, it was found that only 18 percent of organizations rate their LMS reporting systems as "excellent" or "very good" at developing and delivering custom reports. This is a problem continually being addressed by LMS vendors.

The best way to avoid this problem is to assign a dedicated measurement person (as discussed earlier) and let that person develop standardized reports and dashboards that meet the needs of various constituents. Once these reports are established (this may take several months), the LMS reporting system can be configured and customized to generate these reports in a consistent way.

Can the LMS-provided assessment tool be used? Today most LMS systems have fairly robust assessment tools, and I would urge you to use them to ease data integration. As with custom reporting, this is an area of LMS technology that has lagged behind other features—but most LMS vendors now have a focus on this area.

Many organizations use third-party tools (for example, Zoomerang for surveys or Questionmark for more detailed assessments). Although these tools will make assessments more functional, they add the complex step of extracting the data and storing it in the LMS or some other system for analysis, so we recommend using the LMS-provided system first.

Training Analytics and Advanced Reporting

One of the exciting new developments in training technology over the last few years is the advent of training analytics systems. The term "analytics" when applied to training simply means a toolset that enables the training manager to filter, drill and analyze sets of data through dimensions.[3]

Today, the large LMS providers (for example, SumTotal, Saba, Plateau, and Oracle) and many of the smaller companies now offer an analytics module.

These tools deliver tremendous value. For example, suppose the training manager is looking at summary data of learning satisfaction for a new-hire training program. The training manager may want to view that data by session, instructor, and location. He or she then may find that, within one session, the ratings are much higher or lower than another. Then the training manager may decide that he or she would like to do an audience analysis of these results to identify whether certain audiences (for instance, employees from a particular geography) have higher or lower ratings. Although this type of analysis can be performed with a traditional reporting tool, it will require that many custom reports be developed. Analytics tools make the filtering, drilling, and aggregation of data much easier.

We urge companies that are selecting new LMS systems to look hard at the reporting and analytics modules. Although the organization may not realize it at the start, over time, these will be the modules used very frequently. Some of the advanced features that make analytics and reporting more powerful include:

- **Multidimensional Filtering and Drilling.** Clicking on a course within a report and seeing all the sessions of that course; clicking on a manager and seeing all the employees of that manager;

- **Dashboards.** Creating a standard view of information, and then producing a webpage that will display in graphical form for easy viewing by managers or executives;

- **Subscriptions.** Creating a standard report that may run periodically or on some event, and having the system automatically email this report at the end of a course or by month;

- **Charting.** Creating color charts within reports and saving these charts for reuse;

- **Exception Reporting.** Creating reports that show what has NOT occurred, for example, viewing the list of people who registered but did not show up or the list of people who attended but who did not complete a course;

- **Detailed Compliance and Certification Reporting.** Generating detailed reports on the completion of a program, showing not only the date and results, but the version of the program completed, the date this certification may expire, or the number of days before it will expire. This area can become very complex. In some systems, the organization will want the LMS to automatically "decertify" employees when a new version of a course becomes available, so those employees know they have to retake the course; and

- **Integrated Talent Management Reporting.** Looking at many other reports if the company's LMS includes an integrated performance and succession planning system, such as those describing performance ratings, skills gaps, and the relationship between performance ratings and learning results.

In Appendix VI: Training Analytics Specifications, we have included a detailed specification to help identify the right features in a reporting and analytics system. This specification can be used to help select or build an analytics system to support the organization's measurement program.

The KnowledgeAdvisors Solution

One particular solution that bears discussion is the Metrics That Matter™ solution from KnowledgeAdvisors (see Appendix IV: Examples of Learning Measurements for examples of output from KnowledgeAdvisors' system). This product is unique in the marketplace. It provides a complete end-to-end system for the development and delivery of assessments, collection of this data, analysis of the data, and the generation and publishing of custom reports and dashboards. Although the system does not replace the need for LMS reporting, the system can be integrated with most LMS systems.

If you are new to training measurement and do not have an LMS, you should evaluate this solution. KnowledgeAdvisors is an experienced and seasoned solution provider and implements the Kirkpatrick model in an easy-to-use, easy-to-manage environment. The system includes an assessment system, a reporting system, and an analytics system that also integrate with most major LMS systems. It also includes a wide range of pre-built assessment questions to generate the indicator-based measures that track Kirkpatrick and ROI results.

The only limitation with this solution today is that KnowledgeAdvisors is focused primarily on automating the capture of Kirkpatrick measures. The company is expanding its measurement model into a human capital measurement framework, and we expect the tool to incorporate more of the measures in the Impact Measurement Framework in the future.

CLO Dashboard by Zeroed-In Technologies

The other new tool now available to help training organizations measure and monitor their operations is the CLO Dashboard™ by Zeroed-In Technologies (see Figure 9.2). This system serves as an easy-to-use reporting system that enables the CLO or other training manager to establish metrics and alerts, which can refer to data from any data source. The system is particularly useful for organizations that are already collecting data for evaluation in their LMS or may have a data mart with business data, as well as learning data.

In addition to serving as a dashboard tool for data view and display, the system also enables managers to establish custom

Figure 9.2 CLO Dashboard Sample Screen

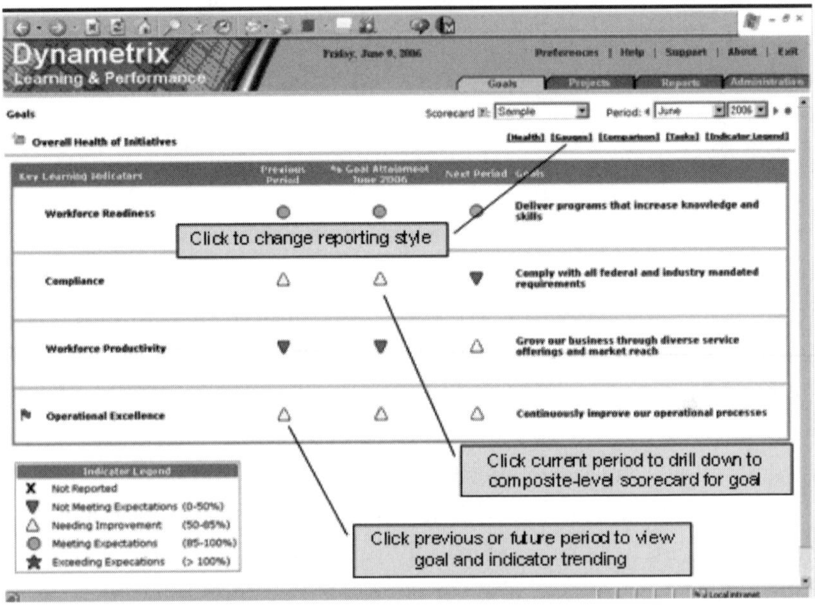

goals, objectives, and measures that can be monitored through the system. While not a full-blown project management system, the system is useful for tracking major L&D initiatives and providing easy-to-use reports that track these projects, as well as other learning program measures (see Figure 9.3).

The system has many of the features already available in standard business intelligence tools, such as those from Business Objects and Cognos. In addition, it is specifically designed for training managers and executives and is priced and packaged for easy implementation.

We recommend that organizations with well-established measurement programs (where data is already being collected in a single database) look at CLO Dashboard as a system to better view and distribute information to enable actionable improvement. Organizations that do not already have a measurement program in place should focus on development of the basic measurement processes first.

Figure 9.3 CLO Dashboard for L&D Goals and Objectives

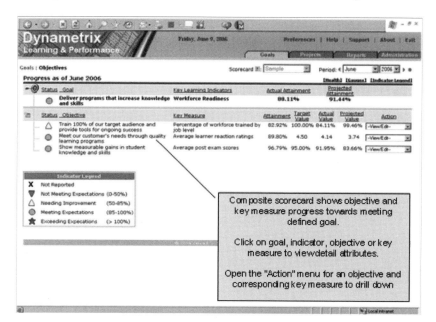

Notes

1. For more information, see *Learning Management Systems 2008: Facts, Practical Analyses, Trends, and Vendor Profiles*. Bersin & Associates/Karen O'Leonard and Josh Bersin, June, 2007. Available at www.bersin.com/lms.

2. For more information, see *Training Analytics: WhatWorks®— What Is Training? How Do You Get Started?* Bersin & Associates/ Josh Bersin, March 2009. Available at www.bersin.com.

3. Descriptive information about the audience or program is often called "dimensional" information in an analytics system.

Chapter Ten

The Journey Forward: Focus on What Matters

While the topic of training measurement seems complex and technical, you can make it easy. Follow a few simple steps and start small. Sophisticated measurement programs evolve over many years.

Here are the key steps to remember.

Consider Your Organization's Business Goals. Build your measurement program around the business goals of your organization. From there, establish a measurement strategy and focus on measuring the things that drive process improvements that drive the business strategy. If your organization is growing, your measurement strategy should measure things that help you gauge your ability to support rapid growth. If your organization is shrinking, you should be measuring efficiency and improvements in productivity.

Focus on Capturing Actionable Information. Measure things you can use. Remember that there is a cost to measurement itself, so the information you gain should be immediately useful. In the development and refinement of your measurement program, make sure you define what decisions you want to make, who your audience will be, and therefore what information you need to make these decisions. By making sure the information you capture is consistent, credible, and specific, you will be gathering actionable information that provides high value to your organization.

Figure 10.1 Training as a Business Support Function

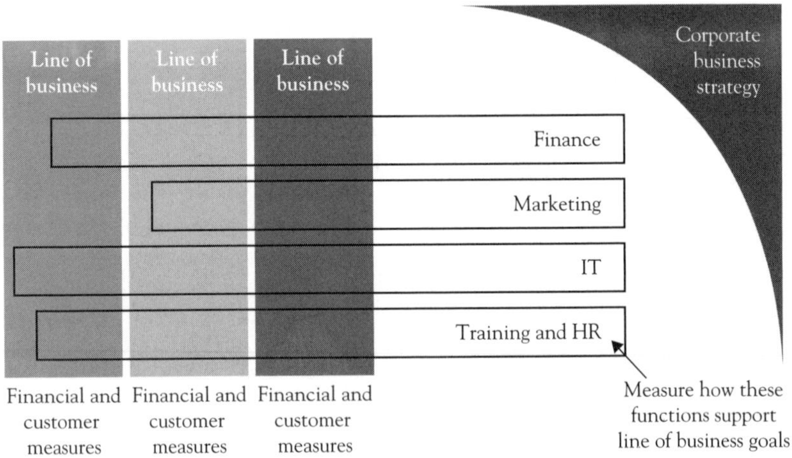

| Line of business | Line of business | Line of business | | Corporate business strategy |

Finance

Marketing

IT

Training and HR

Financial and customer measures | Financial and customer measures | Financial and customer measures

Measure how these functions support line of business goals

Think of Your Organization as a Service-and-Support Function. While training organizations naturally focus on program impact, remember that much of your value to an organization is how you serve the line of business's needs.

Training, similar to HR, marketing, finance, and other functions, serves to support product or line-of-business units. These lines of business have goals to launch products, generate revenue, and deliver customer satisfaction. Your goals and measures should be aligned to **support these goals**. (See Figure 10.1 above.)

Develop and Measure Against a Plan. If you are in the 48 percent of organizations that do not have a written business plan, you should develop one. The process of developing this plan will force business alignment, which in turn will give you a clear set of measures to capture. Your plan should also include goals for efficiency, budget compliance, volumes, and adoption. These measures should be incorporated into your overall measurement strategy.

If You Insist on Using ROI, Compute It Before Developing a Program. While ROI is a valuable exercise, we believe the best possible way to use ROI analysis is to identify the total business value of training *before* you start developing content. In the performance consulting process, you can use signoff forms and other tools to quantify the business problem in advance. These metrics give you the information you need to then validate the value of the program later—in a consistent and repeatable way.

Move Beyond the Kirkpatrick Model. While the Kirkpatrick model is a valuable start, we find that best-practice organizations measure many areas far beyond this model. Consider using satisfaction as a more strategic measure (as did HP) and let business managers tell you how to measure the value of training (an alignment measure). Consider developing a set of customer satisfaction measures and efficiency measures as well.

Remember That Training Measurement Is a Journey, Not a Destination. If you do focus on implementing a measurement process (not a project) you will find, as did HP, Nextel, Sprint, Caterpillar, DAU, Randstad, and every other best-practice organization we spoke with, that this is a journey.

Every best-practice organization we talked with commented that their measurement programs were built over a period of years. Companies such as HP and Caterpillar describe it as a journey (see Figures 10.2 and 10.3). These companies all started with something simple but repeatable and, over time, learned how to capture more and more valuable information.

Use the Impact Framework to Build Your Plan. Review the Impact Measurement Framework and underlying model and identify a few measures you believe best reflect your organization's needs. You may only need a handful of measures to start—in fact most organizations tell us that ultimately, as they evolve their programs, there are a few vitally important measures that become the most valuable in planning and execution. The problem is that you may not know which these are until you start measuring things consistently and seeing which results are most actionable and interesting to your organization.

Figure 10.2 The Measurement Journey at HP

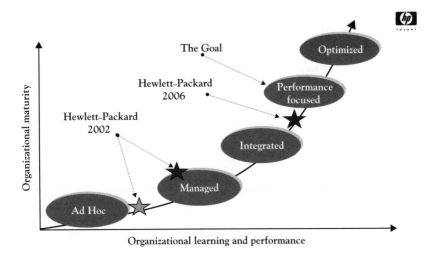

Figure 10.3 The Measurement Journey at Caterpillar

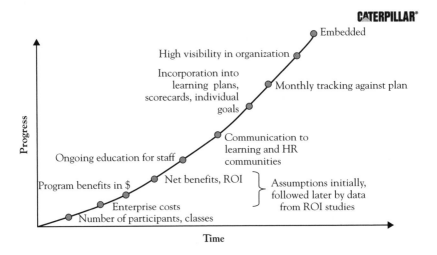

I Hope to Hear from You. Measurement of training is an imperfect science and one that is getting increased focus every year. Each organization tends to focus on approaches that meet the needs of their business, their organization, and their culture. As you apply the research in this book, we are confident that you will identify your own unique and powerful ways to better measure, monitor, and improve your learning and development programs and processes. I am always interested in your successes, lessons learned, and feedback, and hope to hear from you.

Case Study A: Randstad Measures Onboarding

In many organizations, accelerating the time to competency for new employees is a critical driver of profitability. The problem is often exacerbated by high turnover, resulting in lost productivity and opportunity costs while new employees get up to speed.

Although management typically looks to the training or HR department to solve the onboarding challenge, Randstad took a somewhat unique approach. The company devised a new onboarding process for its U.S. operations and aligned it with its global onboarding model. In the new process, line managers, using tools and materials developed by the learning department, drive the onboarding training and are held accountable for the results.

This case study describes Randstad's innovative approach to driving organizational accountability to its onboarding program. Results show significant growth in productivity among new hires in the United States. Randstad's North American team is now facilitating the adoption of the technology and process among its European colleagues.

Randstad Overview

Based in Holland, Randstad is the world's third-largest staffing firm, with $7.85 billion in annual revenues. The company places 250,000 people on a daily basis across seventeen countries throughout Europe, North America, and Japan.

In the past, the company's training initiatives had been largely decentralized, with each country maintaining its own training operations. More recently, however, the company began to realize the significant cost reductions and efficiencies that could be achieved by implementing blended-learning programs and managing these through an enterprise-wide LMS. Toward that end, a global e-learning program office was established within the United States to help lead a companywide rollout of an LMS and develop a new approach to the onboarding process.

The Business Problem

Like many of its competitors, Randstad experiences significant employee turnover. Among the 1,200 staffing agents in North America, turnover is approximately 45 percent, placing a heavy burden on the company's recruiters, trainers, and field managers, as well as affecting the profitability of the company. Randstad's CEO once stated that the company would have generated an additional $110 million in revenues if all agent seats had been filled. One of the main challenges faced by organizations is reducing time to competency among new hires. Line managers often view this challenge as the responsibility of the HR or training team.

At Randstad, staffing agents' performance is judged on a mix of key performance indicators, such as revenue, gross margin dollars, number of positions filled, and displaying the right competencies. Thus, new hires must become productive fast. According to Randstad's hiring profile, most new employees possess no industry-specific knowledge prior to joining the company. This makes the onboarding process a critical piece to achieve the required competencies and productivity.

Each of Randstad's seventeen country operations has maintained its own onboarding program, aligned with a global set of guidelines. The programs have been administered and tracked manually at the individual country level. For example, in the United States from 2003 to 2004, managers used a seventy-two-page, highly structured paper checklist to drive onboarding activities.

From a global perspective, Randstad faced issues such as:

- Inconsistent quality of the onboarding process from manager to manager and country to country;
- Labor-intensive and costly manual processes;
- Lack of a blended-learning approach that could be used to increase efficiencies and reduce expenses;
- Difficulty in tracking and analyzing results globally; and
- The perception that the learning teams, not managers, were the owners and drivers of performance.

Regarding the last point, Randstad's line managers were calling on the training teams to reduce the time-to-competency. This is a common scenario for training managers. A problem is identified, and line managers look to the training team to roll out a new program or course to "fix it." Randstad's L&D organization, however, believed that line managers not only should own their new hires' performance, including the onboarding process, but they also should be held accountable for it.

The Solution

The L&D organization created a new sixteen-week onboarding process in the United State and aligned it with the company's global onboarding model. The process would be driven and owned by line managers. Randstad's LMS (Cornerstone OnDemand) would automate the process and replace the manual procedures. This process would then be used as a template for implementation within Randstad's European countries.

The new onboarding process consisted of a series of learning and on-the-job training activities delivered over a four-month period. The activities break down into the following major categories:

- Manager-facilitated training;
- Instructor-led training;
- Self-study;
- Job shadowing; and
- Manager coaching.

Manager-facilitated training consists of two separate, two-day courses delivered by the employee's district manager. The L&D team creates the instructor and participant guides for the sessions. Topics include Randstad's culture and values, job expectations, sales skills development, and performance and bonus plans. Regional field coordinators schedule the training in the LMS and mark it complete after the training. New hires then evaluate their managers on how well the program was facilitated and how much they believe it will increase their on-the-job effectiveness.

Instructor-led training classes are taught at a central facility by one of the learning team's instructors. Classes are focused on operations, systems, and sales training. Participants self-register for these courses, and the instructors mark them as complete in the LMS. As with the manager-facilitated training, participants evaluate the program's execution and relevance to their jobs.

Self-study programs include online courses and hard-copy manuals on topics, such as Randstad's database and background checking systems, Randstad's organizational structure, and available resources. Some self-study modules serve as prerequisites for face-to-face training or as more advanced learning modules. Learners have self-service access to online modules through the LMS, which tracks their completion and evaluations.

Job shadowing is an activity during which new hires observe veteran employees and managers doing their jobs. This helps new employees learn and practice skills in the actual context of performing the job. This experiential training also supplements classroom training or functions as pre-work to follow-on training. The completion of these activities is tracked in the LMS.

Manager coaching consists of formal and informal feedback sessions between employees and their first-line managers. The manager, aided by a worksheet of behavioral expectations, provides feedback and guidance based on the employee's observed performance on the job and transcripts from the employee's training records. These sessions also afford the employee an opportunity to ask questions and request further training.

Randstad's onboarding process uses a unique blend of formal and informal training methodologies to enable learners to achieve competency. This approach should be used as a model for other companies.

The activities over the four-month onboarding period break down roughly as shown in Figure A1.1.

Figure A1.1 Randstad Onboarding Activities by Month

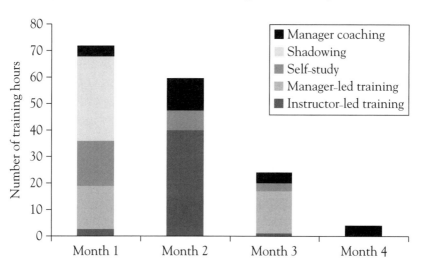

As the figure shows, the volume of training decreases each month as employees transition into their jobs. At the end of each month, employees take a knowledge test reflecting that month's performance objectives. At the end of Month 4, new hires take a comprehensive final examination which, if passed, qualifies them to receive a certificate of completion and recognition from their manager and branch team.

Manager Ownership of the Training

The keys to the new program's success were (1) encouraging managers to own the process and results and (2) enabling managers to develop deeper relationships with their new hires. These were critical keys to achieving greater employee productivity and retention. However, this required a wholesale change in the way managers viewed their roles and the role of training.

Line managers often viewed onboarding as the responsibility of the HR or training team. If new employees were not achieving competency in an adequate time period, training or HR needed to fix the problem.

Randstad's North American L&D team wanted to change this thinking. They believed successful onboarding had to be the responsibility of line managers, in partnership with the training team. With senior executive support and field subject-matter experts (SMEs), the learning team structured the new onboarding process largely around the line managers, who were responsible for conducting the manager-facilitated training events, supporting the appropriate job shadowing activities, and ensuring that new hires were completing their monthly activities and knowledge assessments.

In addition, Randstad's senior executives and learning team continually sent messages that line managers were responsible for onboarding, including communications to new hires that their managers owned the process. New hires were also empowered with the ability to control the pace of their learning through direct access to modules through the LMS.

The transition did not happen overnight. The CLO of Randstad North America noted that it took Randstad several years to change the established thinking in order to have line managers fully own the onboarding process.

Over the last three years, Randstad slowly removed training from driving the process and helped managers take ownership. At the same time, they had to facilitate change management within the training organization itself as they moved from one model to the next. It took some time, but they had to be satisfied with a series of small, incremental steps.

Results

Today, Randstad North America's analytics-driven onboarding process is a model for its operations in other countries. What has really captured the imagination of its European partners is the ability to consistently teach global concepts while reducing training costs and the ability to capture data that can be used to evaluate and improve the process.

The company's LMS plays a vital role in capturing data for each stage of the process. Managers can access employee transcripts and are automatically notified via email when an employee fails to complete a module in the designated time period, making it much easier to track employee progress and training needs. Monthly reports (see Figure A1.2) are sent to Randstad executives and line managers showing how well managers are executing on the process.

Randstad's LMS plays a vital role in capturing data for each stage of the process.

For each employee, the report shows activity completions and assessment scores. Each month, three assessments are given:

- A knowledge check (or Level 2 assessment of knowledge acquired);

Figure A1.2 Example of Randstad Onboarding Measurement in Month 1

Last name	First name	Hire date	Manager's name	Regional director's name	Welcome to Randstad	Building your foundation	Prism self-study L3	Talent acquaint team orient	Getting to know the R.	Understanding Randstadt business	Legal admin and management of 1–9	Recruiting talent	Talent management and retention	Background checks using Randstadt...	Understand/mass customer business	Month 1 agreement knowledge check	Month 1 self-assessment	Month 1 manager
Grant	Carey	11/01/04	Hitchcock	Garbo	x	x			x	x	x	x		x				
Hepburn	Kathy	11/15/04	Owens	Corn	x	x	x	x	x	x	x	x	x	x		93	x	
Lee	Jet	11/22/04	Farrow	Allen	x	x	x	x	x	x	x	x	x	x	x	87	x	
Bassett	Angela	11/22/04	Monroe	Foust	x	x			x	x	x	x	x	x				x

- A learner self-assessment of on-the-job behaviors; and
- A manager's assessment of the learner's on-the-job behaviors.

The reporting functionality makes it easy for executives to sort and view which managers and regions are successfully executing the onboarding process.

Evaluating the New Onboarding Process

Early in the process, Randstad's L&D team determined the goals and measures for evaluating the success of the new onboarding process. Figure A1.3 shows the high-level conceptual framework used for evaluation. This framework is an excellent example of measurement being built into the performance consulting and design process of a program.

Several of the evaluation measures are based on learners' self-assessments. As previously discussed, at the end of each month of

Figure A1.3   Randstad Onboarding Evaluation Framework

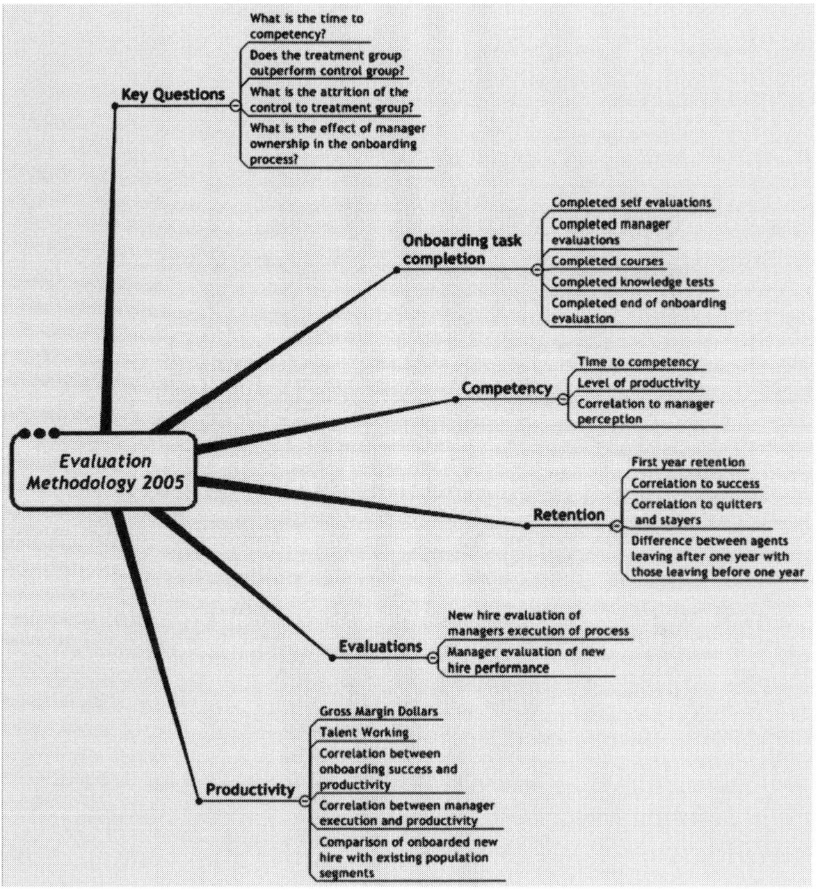

Evaluation Methodology 2005

- **Key Questions**
  - What is the time to competency?
  - Does the treatment group outperform control group?
  - What is the attrition of the control to treatment group?
  - What is the effect of manager ownership in the onboarding process?
- **Onboarding task completion**
  - Completed self evaluations
  - Completed manager evaluations
  - Completed courses
  - Completed knowledge tests
  - Completed end of onboarding evaluation
- **Competency**
  - Time to competency
  - Level of productivity
  - Correlation to manager perception
- **Retention**
  - First year retention
  - Correlation to success
  - Correlation to quitters and stayers
  - Difference between agents leaving after one year with those leaving before one year
- **Evaluations**
  - New hire evaluation of managers execution of process
  - Manager evaluation of new hire performance
- **Productivity**
  - Gross Margin Dollars
  - Talent Working
  - Correlation between onboarding success and productivity
  - Correlation between manager execution and productivity
  - Comparison of onboarded new hire with existing population segments

training, new hires are given an assessment in which they evaluate their own on-the-job behaviors. A learner's self-reported scores on selected measures are shown in Figure A1.4. The figure shows the average scores on each measure before the start of the program and then after the program's completion.

As shown in Figure A1.4, the self-evaluation scores of new hires are consistently higher across all measures after the training is completed—one indication that the training has achieved its desired behavioral goals.

Figure A1.4 Pre- and Post-Evaluations of On-the-Job Performance

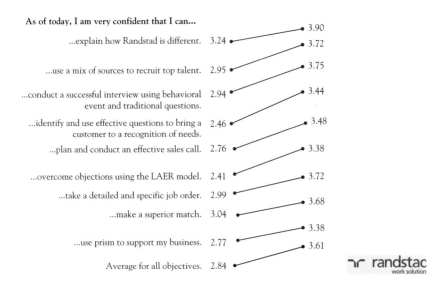

As of today, I am very confident that I can...

...explain how Randstad is different. 3.24 → 3.90 / 3.72

...use a mix of sources to recruit top talent. 2.95 → 3.75

...conduct a successful interview using behavioral event and traditional questions. 2.94 → 3.44

...identify and use effective questions to bring a customer to a recognition of needs. 2.46 → 3.48

...plan and conduct an effective sales call. 2.76 → 3.38

...overcome objections using the LAER model. 2.41 → 3.72

...take a detailed and specific job order. 2.99 → 3.68

...make a superior match. 3.04 → 3.38

...use prism to support my business. 2.77 → 3.61

Average for all objectives. 2.84

ᴨᴄ randstac
work solution

Five to six months after the onboarding program is completed, managers will be given a Kirkpatrick Level 3 assessment to determine how well the learning has transferred to the job in measurable behavioral changes.

Randstad also uses observed performance measures to determine training's impact on productivity. In one analysis conducted in late 2004 (see Figure A1.5), the team compared the performance of nearly five hundred employees who participated

Figure A1.5 Randstad Job Impact Measurements of Onboarding Program

Activity	Control group	Experimental group
Number calls	77%	303%
Number visits	140%	273%
Number prospects in portfolio	26%	108%
Revenues	24%	108%
Gross margin	28%	125%

in the new training program (the "experimental group") with that of approximately four hundred employees hired before the new training was rolled out (the "control group").

The percentages in Figure A1.5 show the speed of growth in productivity across five measures over an eighteen-week period. Among both the control and experimental groups, productivity measures increased over that period. However, the productivity measures for employees who received the new training (the experimental group) grew at a much faster rate. For example, the growth rate in the number of calls made by employees who received the training was nearly four times that of employees who did not receive the new training.

Similarly, the number of client visits, prospects in the portfolio, revenues, and gross margin also increased at a much faster rate among those who received the new onboarding training versus employees who were hired prior to the training. The analysis factors out variances in previous skills and experience, as one might expect a new hire with no previous skills to develop at a much faster rate than someone with prior experience.

Randstad has found that, through the new onboarding process, new hires are now able to achieve a baseline level of competency in just sixteen weeks, a shorter timeframe than previously observed. Onboarding training not only developed skills, but increased the speed of developing new skills.

Randstad is understandably delighted with these results and expects even more significant results from this year's process improvements. The data show that the new onboarding process has been extremely effective in increasing new employees' rates of productivity. The ability to obtain this data is a huge leap for the company for which previous manual methods made gathering and analyzing this type of data impossible. Randstad's LMS provides the capability to evaluate the results at multiple levels within the organization, so that corrective procedures can be put in place where necessary to improve the effectiveness of the process.

Lessons Learned

Through this process, Randstad's L&D team has learned a number of key lessons. These can be summed up as follows.

Be an Agent for Change. The training team needs to get out of the mode of reacting to requests and place an emphasis on engaging the organization around shared responsibility. Although it may be easier to just roll out a new course to pacify line managers, training managers need to know whether this is really the right thing to do.

Demonstrate Business Impact. One of the keys to the program's success was the ability to show its business impact. The team compared data showing the performance of new hires who completed the onboarding process versus the performance of those hired before the new process to demonstrate productivity gains. This was a surefire way to gain executive attention and to drive adherence to the process.

Use Data to Hold Managers and the Training Organization Accountable. The process must be able to report data that holds managers accountable for results and provides the training organization with a means for taking corrective action. Reports have to provide meaningful and credible data in an easy-to-understand format.

Create a Roadmap. Randstad's L&D team created a roadmap of major milestones comprising small incremental steps. The team has worked consistently toward their goals over the last three years, and they continue to iterate and improve on the process.

Next Steps

Going forward, Randstad is preparing to partner with those countries that are looking forward to using technology and blended learning to support their onboarding processes. Randstad refined its global implementation plan for its operations in the remaining countries.

In the United States, Randstad plans to take its existing process one step further. As part of the 2005 process, new hires will rate their managers on the quality of the onboarding process, and managers will be compensated based on these ratings. A sample of the questions and recent results are shown in Figure A1.6.

Middle- and senior-level managers' merit increases will be, in part, tied to their onboarding effectiveness, because coaching and employee development are compensable factors in the annual appraisal process. Randstad's managing directors of operations have agreed that investing in the onboarding process is critical to their success, and an important component to that success is having managers drive and own the process. The CLO of Randstad North America commented: "This shows a clear sense of responsibility for the quality of the onboarding process. We are all committed to evolving the process in order to further improve our results."

Randstad's onboarding measurement is an excellent example a training measurement program that is aligned, actionable, pragmatic, and business-centric.

Figure A1.6 Learner Evaluation of Manager Performance

How many hours did your District Manager (DM) spend with you performing sales activities (calls and visits)?	
None	16%
1–5 hours	33%
6–10 hours	22%
11–15 hours	9%
16–20 hours	7%
More than 20 hours	12%
Did your branch manager set clear activity and results expectations with you?	
Yes	79%
No	0%
Somewhat	21%
Approximately how many client visits has your branch manager attended with you?	
0 visits	10%
1–5 visits	40%
6–10 visits	19%
11–15 visits	12%
16–20 visits	6%
More than 20 visits	12%
How effective was your DM in your overall onboarding process? (mean rating 1–5 scale)	4.3
How effective was your branch manager in supporting your onboarding process? (mean rating 1–5 scale)	4.4

Case Study B: HP Develops an Integrated Measurement Process

HP has a global L&D organization that works in a federated model[1] with business analysts who work with each major organizational unit. The central organization is responsible for tools, processes, and support for centers of expertise in leadership, sales, technical, and professional curricula. Functional and business-unit-specific training is done in business unit training groups.

HP Measurement Goals

In 2002, HP set out on a goal to standardize and rationalize its training measurement process. The goal of this program was to develop the right level of actionable data to help HP address four challenges, as shown in Figure A2.1:

- Provide top-level managers with information about their training investments that would help them understand how their people and support process were aligned with strategic business initiatives. As described in the beginning of this study, this is actionable information targeted at executives.
- Provide reporting that would help business units ensure that training was aligned with strategic business initiatives and give business and learning managers information to help them understand how aligned they were or were not. This

Figure A2.1 HP's Measurement Goals and Strategy

"alignment goal" is the goal of optimizing the learning port-folio. This is information targeted at line and L&D managers.

- Provide L&D managers with detailed reporting on program effectiveness, so they can continuously improve the learning experience. This is information targeted toward the L&D staff and operational teams.

- Provide the entire organization with process and operational information that would help the local and centralized L&D organizations improve their efficiency.

HP Systematic Approach

HP took a very systematic approach to this problem. The company developed a process for identifying the measurement requirements, then developed the surveys and instruments needed and mapped these to the process. HP uses this to build and deploy training.

As Figure A2.2 shows, HP designed the process up-front to capture summative Level 3 and Level 4 data (business-impact

Figure A2.2 Research: What Do Organizations Measure?

The solution lifecycle: start with the end in mind...

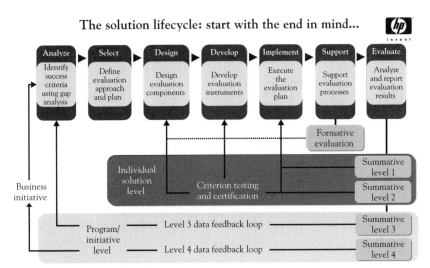

and job-impact data) that could be fed back into the performance management (called "gap analysis" here) process. The company wanted the more granular, program-level data (Levels 1 and 2) to be able to feed directly back into the process for program design and delivery.

The value of this approach is that it enabled HP to build a measurement process that can be implemented across all training units within HP. This collaborative approach, although slower to deploy, allowed HP to build a process and toolset that could be used enterprise-wide with high levels of adoption and success.

The team set up an evaluation *steering committee* composed of "evaluation champions" from each of the federated business units. Over a period of months, this team brainstormed approaches, identified what would work in their businesses, and developed an approach that they could all adopt. HP also initiated an "e-brownbag" series, so that individuals throughout the HP learning organization could start to understand various best practices in measurement and evaluation.

Designed to Deliver Actionable Information

A key best practice that HP adopted was clearly defining up-front what actionable information was desired. The measurement solution must fit with assigned roles within HP. As Figure A2.3 illustrates, the goal was to integrate evaluation into the front end of program design, not only at the back end.

A critical step in this initiative was to understand how measurement would fit into each of the established roles in HP's L&D process. Figure A2.4 illustrates HP's competency development roadmap for professional careers (on the horizontal axis). On the vertical axis, it shows the four key learning roles in the organization.

As the figure shows, the business consultants and learning solution owners (instructional designers and program development team) are responsible for identifying program success criteria.

The business consultant (performance consultant) builds an evaluation plan. As described earlier in this book (see Chapter 5: Implementation: The Seven-Step Training Measurement Process),

Figure A2.3 What Is Frequently Measured: 2006 Versus 2004

And supported by defined roles   *hp*

Task \ Role	Solution owner
Gain sponsor agreement	Identify solution success metrics with project sponsor
Develop evaluation approach and plan	Develop plan to design/develop evaluation instruments
Implement the plan	Enlist stakeholder support in the evaluation implementation plan
Analyze the results	Analyze evaluation results; define action plans
Act on results	Proceed with actions where root cause is related to course or content
Communicate findings	Communicate evaluation results quarterly to key stakeholders

- Using a project management approach

- Developing the evaluation plan at the front end

- Executing a closed loop process

- Making the results visible: good or bad

Figure A2.4 Training Spending on Measurement

HP's roadmap for building competency

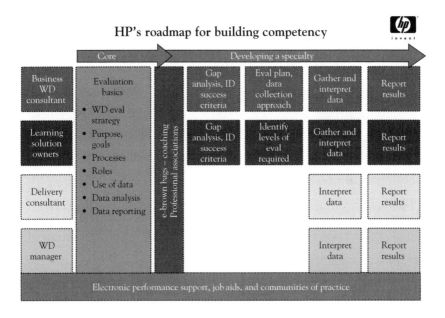

the performance consultant should gather detailed business case and root-cause information in his or her discovery process. Armed with this information, he or she can determine what program-specific success criteria are appropriate to measure.

The learning solution owners (designer and developer) should also understand these success criteria and the levels of evaluation required. They will likely be building assessments into the body of the course.

The delivery consultant will be viewing and interpreting results. (Some of the results indicate his or her effectiveness in program delivery.)

Finally, the L&D manager will view final results.

This approach helps each person in the L&D process to clearly understand his or her role in the measurement process.

HP Solution: Standard Evaluation and Indicators

The next step in HP's journey was the development of a standard evaluation and set of indicators, which they call the HP "data model." The company performed a psychometric evaluation and looked at many variables to come up with a very simple twelve-question evaluation that met the following criteria:

- It was very easy to implement;
- It had very few questions, making it possible to be used consistently;
- It gave business owners and L&D managers the ability to quickly view the program strengths and weaknesses in a graphical format; and
- It delivered actionable information that could be used to improve programs going forward.

The first version of the data model is shown in Figure A2.5: The HP Evaluation Data Model. There were twelve questions asked, indicated by the boxes on the outer edge of this diagram. (The actual survey instrument for instructor-led programs is shown

Figure A2.5 The HP Evaluation Data Model

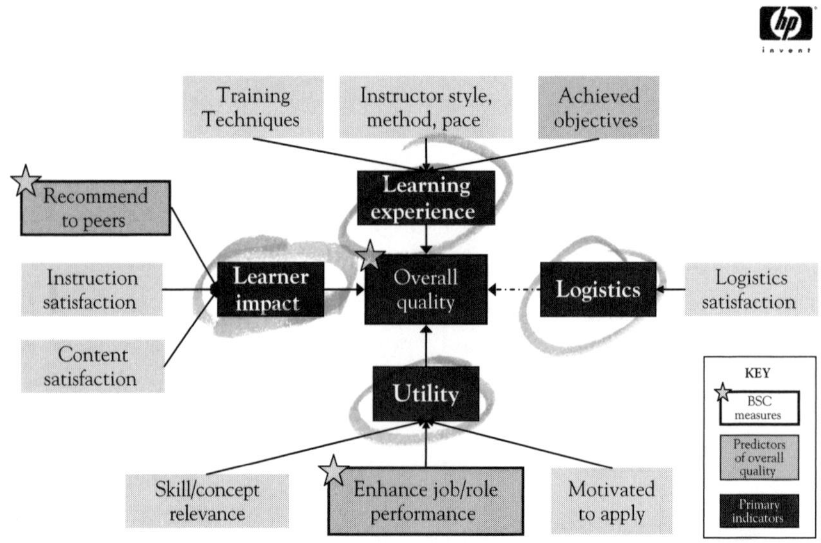

in Figure A2.7: HP Evaluation Instrument.) Three questions cover the learning experience, three questions cover learner impact, three questions cover utility, and one question covers logistics. There is one overall quality question.

From these twelve basic questions (asked in the end-of-course surveys), HP then derived five indicators that were averages of the questions surrounding them. Learning experience, for example, is the arithmetic average of training techniques, instructor style/method/pace, and achieved objectives.

The "overall quality" measure in the center was the final question in the survey.

One of the interesting findings from HP's work was that overall quality was directly related to three other measures:

- Did the course achieve its stated objectives?
- Would learners recommend the course to their peers?
- How well did the course enhance their jobs and role performances?

HP found that these indicators are, in essence, the "drivers" of the overall satisfaction measure.

Graphical View of Program Impact

One of the results of this simple but powerful approach is how the data can be viewed and distributed. Once someone is familiar with this graphical layout, it is easy to "score" programs with green, yellow, or red indicators. For example, a sample program (shown in Figure A2.6) scored high in learning experience and logistics, moderate in learning impact, and low in utility. This would be an example of a program that was flawlessly designed and executed, but suffered from a lack of performance consulting up-front.

As HP measured more and more programs, the criteria for green, yellow, and red became clearer.

Figure A2.6 HP Sample Program Evaluation Dashboard

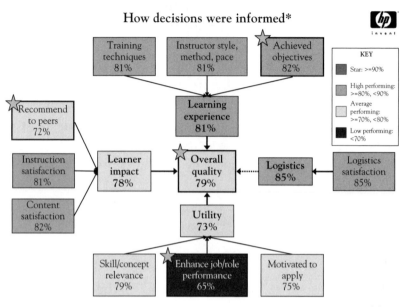

How decisions were informed*

*Not actual data

HP Measurement Survey

Figure A2.7 is an illustration of the HP survey tool. It is simple, easy to understand, and easy to complete.

Lessons Learned

Organizations can learn many things from HP's measurement journey.

- First, HP set out clear objectives for measurement up-front;
- Second, HP designed a process that integrates with their overall development and delivery model;
- Third, HP started simply and developed a repeatable process that generated consistent and easy-to-analyze data;

Figure A2.7 HP Evaluation Instrument

Workforce Development and Organization Effectiveness
FY'05 Classroom ILT Course Evaluation

invent

Instructions: Please be sure to fill in the information fields provided below, as well as the demographics of Level, Region, Business and Vendor, as all are critical information for reporting purposes.

Fill in bubbles like this: ●
To change a response,
cross it out and mark another.

Demographics

Course Name: ▮   **Date:** [   ] 2 0 0 5

Course Number: [   ] **Your Name: (optional)** [   ]

Instructor: [   ] **Vendor:** [   ]

Location: [   ] **Business:** ○ TSG   ○ Worldwide Operations

Level: ○ Individual Contributor (IC)   ○ IC Leading a Project Team   ○ Manager   ○ CSG   ○ Infrastructure

Region: ○ Americas   ○ Asia - Pacific   ○ EMEA   ○ Japan   ○ IPG   ○ Channel Partner
                                                                    ○ PSG   ○ Non-HP Employee

Course Feedback

	Strongly Disagree	Disagree	Neutral	Agree	Strongly Agree
1. The training techniques used to teach the different skills/concepts maximized my learning.	○	○	○	○	○
2. The skills/concepts taught are highly relevant to the demands of my job/role.	○	○	○	○	○
3. The instructor(s) style, methods, and pace helped me to learn.	○	○	○	○	○
4. What I have learned will significantly enhance my job/role performance.	○	○	○	○	○
5. I feel strongly motivated to apply these new skills/concepts in my job/role.	○	○	○	○	○
6. I believe that this program achieved its stated objectives.	○	○	○	○	○
7. I would highly recommend this learning solution to my peers.	○	○	○	○	○

8. I would describe my overall satisfaction with the logistics supporting this course to be:
    ○ Dissatisfied   ○ Somewhat Dissatisfied   ○ Somewhat Satisfied   ○ Satisfied   ○ Completely Satisfied

9. I would describe my overall level of satisfaction with the instruction provided in the course to be:
    ○ Dissatisfied   ○ Somewhat Dissatisfied   ○ Somewhat Satisfied   ○ Satisfied   ○ Completely Satisfied

10. I would describe my overall satisfaction with the program content to be:
    ○ Dissatisfied   ○ Somewhat Dissatisfied   ○ Somewhat Satisfied   ○ Satisfied   ○ Completely Satisfied

11. I would rate the quality of this learning solution to be: ○ Poor   ○ Fair   ○ Good   ○ Very Good   ○ Excellent

12. What comments do you have about any aspect of the course (instructor, content, etc.)?

● Fourth, HP learned and iterated on the process as they analyzed more and more data; and

● Finally, HP viewed and invested in their measurement program as an ongoing process that can be improved and modified over time.

HP's experience is an example of a process that started with the end-point in mind, enlisted the support of all managers and training personnel in the process, mapped the use of the process against each job role, and then implemented a repeatable process that enabled the team to analyze quickly. It is an excellent example of a process that any large organization could adopt.

Note

1. For more information, see The High-Impact Learning Organization: WhatWorks® in *The Management, Organization, and Governance of Corporate Training.* Bersin & Associates, June 2005. Available at www.bersin.com.

Appendix III

Research: The State of Training Measurement Today

As part of this research effort, in 2006 we surveyed research members to understand current trends, issues, and benchmarks in training measurement. This survey was a follow-up to a similar survey we conducted in the summer of 2004.

The survey was sent to CLOs, directors, and senior managers of training throughout North America, and we received 136 detailed responses.

In general, this survey illustrates the relative immaturity of measurement in many organizations and the need for easier, more business-focused measurement solutions in corporate training. It illustrates the challenge that organizations have in general planning and alignment, which, in turn, leads to challenges in measurement.

What Do Training Organizations Consider Important?

One of the first questions asked was what measures organizations consider important, as shown in Figure A3.1.

As the figure indicates, organizations are very interested in understanding impact: job impact, business impact, and specific business impacts. These measures are considered important because they help the organization demonstrate value and refine programs to better drive results.

Figure A3.1 Research Results: What Measures Are Considered Important

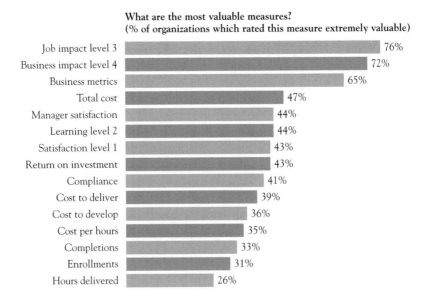

What are the most valuable measures?
(% of organizations which rated this measure extremely valuable)

Measure	%
Job impact level 3	76%
Business impact level 4	72%
Business metrics	65%
Total cost	47%
Manager satisfaction	44%
Learning level 2	44%
Satisfaction level 1	43%
Return on investment	43%
Compliance	41%
Cost to deliver	39%
Cost to develop	36%
Cost per hours	35%
Completions	33%
Enrollments	31%
Hours delivered	26%

A significant number of organizations (47 percent) consider cost a critical measure, but interestingly 53 percent do **NOT** consider cost a valuable measure. This is somewhat surprising, considering that training is, in fact, a cost center and, without understanding the nature of these costs, it is impossible to measure ROI or improve efficiency.

Another interesting finding is that only 44 percent believe that learning results (Level 2) are extremely valuable and only 43 percent believe that satisfaction is extremely valuable. These two foundational measures of the Kirkpatrick model are clearly limited in value. This is not surprising, given the fact that corporate training is a business performance improvement function (not an education function) and that measures should focus more on performance than learning. It further justifies the motivation for Bersin & Associates' Impact Measurement Framework.

What Do Training Organizations Actually Measure?

Understanding the measurement desires, we then wanted to understand the current state of measurement. Unfortunately, the current state of measurement is almost inverse to the perceptions of value. Organizations are frequently measuring things that they do not see as highly valuable.

As Figure A3.2 shows, most organizations focus on measuring standard course operations: enrollments, and completion. Level 1 surveys are now very widely used (81 percent of organizations use these regularly).

A very small number of organizations routinely measure ROI, business impact, or job impact. This further supports our hypothesis (explained in detail in this book) that training organizations are looking for help creating easy-to-implement processes for measuring impact. The Bersin Impact Measurement Framework is designed to help in this area.

Figure A3.2 Research: What Do Organizations Measure?

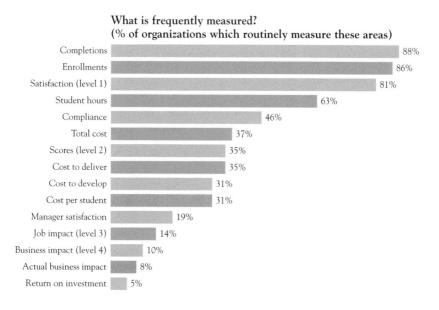

What is frequently measured?
(% of organizations which routinely measure these areas)

Completions	88%
Enrollments	86%
Satisfaction (level 1)	81%
Student hours	63%
Compliance	46%
Total cost	37%
Scores (level 2)	35%
Cost to deliver	35%
Cost to develop	31%
Cost per student	31%
Manager satisfaction	19%
Job impact (level 3)	14%
Business impact (level 4)	10%
Actual business impact	8%
Return on investment	5%

Figure A3.3 What Is Frequently Measured: 2006 Versus 2004

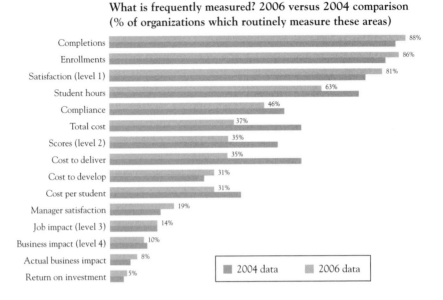

What is frequently measured? 2006 versus 2004 comparison
(% of organizations which routinely measure these areas)

Completions	88%
Enrollments	86%
Satisfaction (level 1)	81%
Student hours	63%
Compliance	46%
Total cost	37%
Scores (level 2)	35%
Cost to deliver	35%
Cost to develop	31%
Cost per student	31%
Manager satisfaction	19%
Job impact (level 3)	14%
Business impact (level 4)	10%
Actual business impact	8%
Return on investment	5%

■ 2004 data   ■ 2006 data

The other interesting finding (which we consider disappointing) is that only one-third of organizations or fewer measure cost. Thirty-seven percent measure the total cost of a training program, and only 31 percent measure development cost or cost per student. This is an indicator that many training organizations are not able to focus their time on operational excellence and efficiency.

When comparing this data with the results from our 2004 study (Figure A3.3), little major progress was found. In almost every high-value area, the percent of organizations that routinely measure these areas is lower in 2006 than it was in 2004. While the samples were not identical, we believe this indicates that, in general, there is a similar level of frustration in learning measurement today as there was in 2004.

Budgets for Training Measurement

Respondents were asked to estimate what percent of their companies' total training budget is spent on measurement, as seen in Figure A3.4. Our research shows that, without a dedicated

Figure A3.4 Training Spending on Measurement

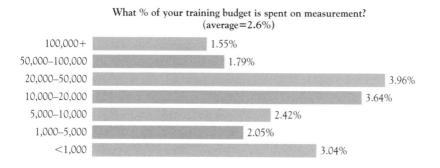

Legend:
- 5–9% on measurement
- 2–5% on measurement
- 1–2% on measurement
- <1% on measurement
- >10% on measurement

resource, training measurement is difficult to implement in a consistent way.

The result was an overall average of 2.6 percent of budget spent on training measurement.

However, this reflects a high standard deviation of results. In fact, one-third of companies surveyed spend far more than the average, and 42 percent spend far below the average. There are a large number of companies (nearly half) who spend almost nothing and there are a small number of companies (16 percent) who invest heavily—spending 5 percent to 10 percent or more.

Looking at the spending by organization size, as seen in Figure A3.5, spending is, in fact, fairly evenly distributed. Very large

Figure A3.5 Spending on Measurement as a Function of Organization Size

What % of your training budget is spent on measurement?
(average=2.6%)

Organization Size	Spending
100,000+	1.55%
50,000–100,000	1.79%
20,000–50,000	3.96%
10,000–20,000	3.64%
5,000–10,000	2.42%
1,000–5,000	2.05%
<1,000	3.04%

organizations can leverage their dedicated resources across a large audience, so their percentages are low. But small- and mid-sized organizations all spend to some degree, so we believe the findings indicate that companies of any size can afford to spend 3 to 5 percent of their budgets on measurement if they choose to do so.

The Importance of a Business Plan

An important factor in an organization's ability to measure training is how well they manage the overall planning and budgeting process. The business planning process is instrumental in measuring alignment. In this survey, only half (52 percent) of respondents stated that they have a written business plan for budgets, volumes, and program deliverables. (See Figure A3.6.) Of course, without such a plan it is impossible to measure "results versus plan."

This somewhat surprisingly low number of organizations that have a business plan led us to hypothesize that the organizations without a business plan are likely to be doing less measurement. In fact, this is true.

Figure A3.6 Is There a Written Plan for the Training Organization?

Do you have a written business plan
for budgets, volumes and program deliverables?

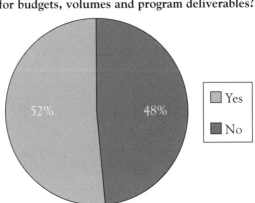

- Organizations *with* a written business plan spend 60 percent more on training measurement than those without a business plan;

- Organizations *with* a written business plan are twice as likely to measure alignment through executive reviews and steering committees than those without a business plan;

- Organizations *without* a business plan are four times more likely to see a need for significantly higher spending on measurement than they are spending today; and

- Organizations *without* a business plan are three times more likely to rate themselves "poor" or "marginal" in their overall success at measuring the effectiveness and efficiency of training.

How Do Organizations Measure Alignment?

We specifically asked organizations to explain more about how they measure and manage business alignment. Here the answers were again somewhat disappointing:

- Sixty percent of organizations measure alignment by their ability to "meet their budget";

- Fifty-four percent of organizations measure alignment through an annual executive review of their operations (this seems very low);

- Forty-one percent of organizations measure alignment by their ability to "deliver programs on time";

- Thirty-nine percent of organizations measure alignment by their ability to "meet learner satisfaction targets";

- Twenty-four percent of organizations measure alignment by their ability to "maintain job satisfaction in the training department"; and

- Fifteen percent of organizations measure alignment by their ability to "meet target volumes delivered."

These results indicate that training organizations do not have good measures in place to make sure they are consistently aligned with corporate priorities.

Training managers and executives were then asked to relate what techniques they use to make sure they are staying close to ever-changing business requirements (an alignment issue). The results were similarly disappointing, as seen by Figure A3.7.

In our High-Impact Learning Organization[1] research, it was found very conclusively that organizations with high levels of effectiveness and efficiency focus heavily on a three-tier governance process. This includes an executive steering committee, a series of learning "councils" (which often include line of business representation) and a series of operational teams (which work together on internal training processes). We also found

Figure A3.7 How Do Organizations Stay Aligned with Changing Business Needs?

Technique	% of organizations that use this process regularly
Regular meetings with individual line managers.	61%
Quarterly program review with line managers (i.e., steering committee).	22%
Compliance with the standardized L&D business plan.	33% (Only 52% even have a plan, so more than one-third of these do not regularly measure compliance with this plan.)
A dashboard of standard operational measures for the training function.	28%

a significant correlation between organizations that implement effective measurement programs and those rated high in effectiveness and efficiency.

Training organizations with high levels of effectiveness and efficiency focus heavily on a **three-tier governance process**.

The research from this study further reinforces these findings by illustrating how often training departments do not have a detailed operational plan (nearly half) and how even those with a plan do not measure themselves against the plan on a regular basis.

Why, in fact, are training organizations having such a difficult time with such operational measurements? One problem may be the lack of performance consulting processes in place.

The Role of Performance Consulting

Because we know that performance consulting is such an important factor in effectiveness, efficiency, and measurement, respondents were asked in this survey whether or not they had a performance consulting role. See Figure A3.8 for the results.

Performance consulting is such an important factor in effectiveness, efficiency, and measurement.

Figure A3.8 Does the Organization Have a Performance Consulting Role?

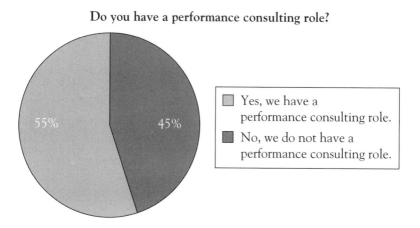

Do you have a performance consulting role?

55%   45%

☐ Yes, we have a performance consulting role.

■ No, we do not have a performance consulting role.

Again the findings were somewhat disappointing—almost half of the organizations in this survey do not have such a role (45 percent). These organizations without a performance consulting role, on average, spend 20 percent less on measurement. Organizations with written business plans are three times as likely to have a performance consulting role, illustrating that, in general, more sophisticated and business-focused learning organizations have all three processes in place. These organizations:

- Have a written business and operational plan;
- Have a performance consulting role that works closely with lines of business; and
- Spend above average on training measurement and are more satisfied with their measurement processes.

Satisfaction with LMS Systems

In this survey, we also asked organizations how satisfied they were with their LMS systems. As seen in Figure A3.9, only about

Figure A3.9 How Well Does the LMS Support Training Measurement Needs?

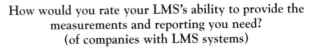

How would you rate your LMS's ability to provide the measurements and reporting you need? (of companies with LMS systems)

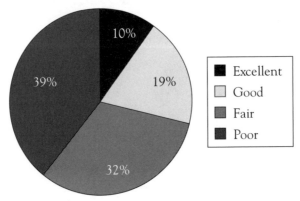

two-thirds of the organizations responding had a full-functioning LMS system. We specifically asked those with LMS systems how well the systems were helping to facilitate the measurement process. As with other research we have performed in this area, the results were relatively low.

Only 29 percent of respondents stated that their LMS was excellent or good at providing the desired measurements and reporting capabilities, and 39 percent rated their systems "poor." As described in this study, this is due to several factors:

- Lack of data standards;
- Lack of measurement process;
- Poor content integration; and
- The difficulty of using the LMS reporting system itself.

As discussed throughout this book, many of these problems can be solved through the implementation of a sound measurement program—some can only be solved by an investment in data standards, integration, and more advanced LMS features.

Is Enough Being Spent on Training Measurement?

Finally, we asked respondents whether they were spending enough or should they be spending more. As expected, and shown in Figure A3.10, almost all respondents felt they should be spending more.

A full 82 percent of organizations feel they should be spending "more" or "much more," and almost one-third (31 percent) feel they should be spending "much more." In general, when talking with training managers individually, we found that the biggest challenges they face are not lack of budget but, rather, a difficulty understanding precisely how to implement a measurement program and, from there, build the business case for the budget.

Figure A3.10 Are You Spending Enough on Training Measurement?

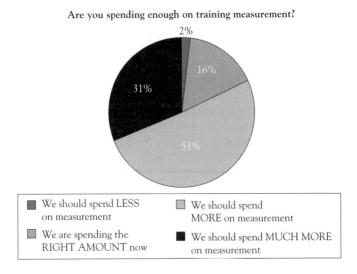

Are you spending enough on training measurement?

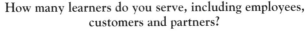

■ We should spend LESS on measurement	□ We should spend MORE on measurement
□ We are spending the RIGHT AMOUNT now	■ We should spend MUCH MORE on measurement

Demographics from the Survey

This survey came from a broad number of organizations in a wide range of sizes and industries, as seen in Figures A3.11 and A3.12.

Figure A3.11 2006 Survey Demographics: Organization Size

How many learners do you serve, including employees, customers and partners?

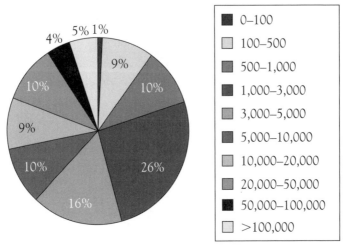

■ 0–100	
□ 100–500	
■ 500–1,000	
■ 1,000–3,000	
■ 3,000–5,000	
■ 5,000–10,000	
□ 10,000–20,000	
■ 20,000–50,000	
■ 50,000–100,000	
□ >100,000	

Figure A3.12 2006 Survey: Industry

What is your organization's industry

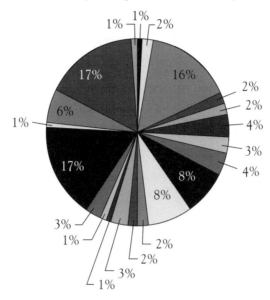

■ Utilities	■ Manufacturing (durable)
☐ Aerospace	▨ Manufacturing (non–durable)
▨ Banking/finance	
■ Business services/consulting	■ Media/entertainment
☐ Construction	☐ Nonprofit
■ Education	▨ Oil and gas/mining
☐ Government (federal, including military)	■ Other
	☐ Pharmaceuticals
▨ Government (state/local)	▨ Retail
■ Healthcare	■ Technology (computers, software, ISP, etc.)
☐ Insurance	
▨ Legal	▨ Transportation

We did not find any significant trends in spending, maturity, or measurement sophistication across these different organization sizes or industries. Interestingly, the challenge of developing and implementing a consistent and powerful measurement program haunts small, medium, and large organizations equally.

Note

1. For more information, see The High-Impact Learning Organization: WhatWorks® in *The Management, Organization, and Governance of Corporate Training.* Bersin & Associates, June 2005. Available at www.bersin.com.

Examples of Learning Measurements

The figures in this appendix illustrate the best practices of different measurement approaches and methodologies used by a variety of companies. These should provide ideas and insights into developing a measurement program and specific actionable reports.

Caterpillar University ROI Analyses

Caterpillar has a very well-refined planning and measurement process, which includes measurement of ROI. Although Caterpillar tries to measure ROI. Their ROI process is used to help "rank" and "qualify" programs against each other, rather than to provide real economic cost-justification. See Figures A4.1, A4.2, and A4.3 for some samples from Caterpillar.

While these charts show Caterpillar's focus on ROI and cost-justification, these are only one of many measures the organization uses to monitor and measure training investments.

DAU: Business-Focused Approach

The Defense Acquisition University (DAU) is a very large training organization responsible for training all federal and civilian procurement personnel. Its corporate university is managed and measured closely, and its CLO uses many of the measurement areas in the Bersin & Associates Learning Impact Measurement Framework. See Figures A4.4 and A4.5 for two of their scorecards.

Figure A4.1 Caterpillar ROI Strategy

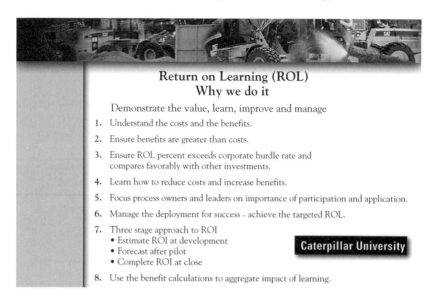

Return on Learning (ROL)
Why we do it

Demonstrate the value, learn, improve and manage

1. Understand the costs and the benefits.

2. Ensure benefits are greater than costs.

3. Ensure ROL percent exceeds corporate hurdle rate and compares favorably with other investments.

4. Learn how to reduce costs and increase benefits.

5. Focus process owners and leaders on importance of participation and application.

6. Manage the deployment for success – achieve the targeted ROL.

7. Three stage approach to ROI
   • Estimate ROI at development
   • Forecast after pilot
   • Complete ROI at close

   Caterpillar University

8. Use the benefit calculations to aggregate impact of learning.

Figure A4.2 Caterpillar Sample ROI Results

Return on learning–improvements in performance

Program	Primary CSFs	Participants 2005	Net benefits (mil)	Participants 2006	Net benefits (mil)
1. Performance management training	People	3,122	$10.1	1,000	$3.2
2. Knowledge sharing	All	41,496	$11.1	41,000	$12.7
3. Pro series/sales effectiveness	Product distribution	5,000	$15.7	7,000	$22.0
4. Making great leaders	All	1,569	$9.9	1,300	$8.2
5. Succeeding in supervision	All	196	$1.1	800	$4.3
6. Business acumen	All	459	$0.4	800	$0.7
7. Change management	All	705	$0.9	1,000	$1.4
8. Safety	People	14,064	$7.6	22,000	$11.8
9. Quality	Quality			2,000	$13.0
10. Engineering	Product. quality	552	$7.2	800	$10.4
11. Curricula for manufacturing	Quality			2000	$11.0
Total		67,163	$64.1	79,700	$98.7

Figure A4.3 Caterpillar Sample Efficiency Measures

Return on learning-improvements in efficiency

Process/system	Metric	Number 2004	Savings (mil)	Number 2005	Savings (mil)
1. E-learning vs. instructor-led	Orders	301,720	$30.2	350,000	$35
2. Sametime vs. physical meeting					
a. Time	Sessions	380,000	$38	550,000	$55
b. Travel costs	Documented $		$4.8		$9.5
3. Centralized development vs. by business units					
• Leadership programs	Business units	10	$0.5	5	$0.3
• Saftey	Business units	10	$1	10	$1
• Business acumen progress	Business units	2	$0.1		
Total savings			$74.9		$101.1

Figure A4.4 DAU Program Scorecard

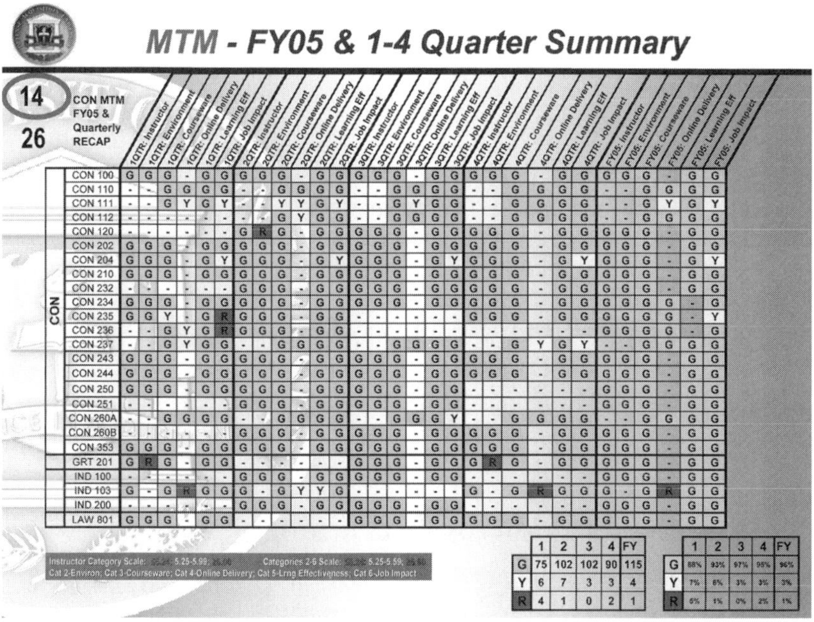

MTM - FY05 & 1-4 Quarter Summary

14 / 26 — CON MTM FY05 & Quarterly RECAP

		1QTR: Instructor	1QTR: Environment	1QTR: Courseware	1QTR: Online Delivery	1QTR: Learning Eff	1QTR: Job Impact	2QTR: Instructor	2QTR: Environment	2QTR: Courseware	2QTR: Online Delivery	2QTR: Learning Eff	2QTR: Job Impact	3QTR: Instructor	3QTR: Environment	3QTR: Courseware	3QTR: Online Delivery	3QTR: Learning Eff	3QTR: Job Impact	4QTR: Instructor	4QTR: Environment	4QTR: Courseware	4QTR: Online Delivery	4QTR: Learning Eff	4QTR: Job Impact	FY05: Instructor	FY05: Environment	FY05: Courseware	FY05: Online Delivery	FY05: Learning Eff	FY05: Job Impact
CON	CON 100	G	G	G	-	G	G	G	G	G	-	G	G	G	G	G	-	G	G	G	G	G	-	G	G	G	G	G	-	G	G
CON	CON 110	-	-	G	G	G	G	-	-	G	G	G	G	-	-	G	G	G	G	-	-	G	G	G	G	-	-	G	G	G	G
CON	CON 111	-	-	G	Y	G	Y	-	-	Y	Y	G	Y	-	-	G	Y	G	G	-	-	G	G	G	G	-	-	G	Y	G	Y
CON	CON 112	-	-	-	-	-	-	-	-	G	Y	G	G	-	-	G	G	G	G	-	-	G	G	G	G	-	-	G	G	G	G
CON	CON 120	-	-	-	-	-	-	G	R	G	-	G	G	G	G	G	-	G	G	G	G	G	-	G	G	G	G	G	-	G	G
CON	CON 202	G	G	G	-	G	G	G	G	G	-	G	G	G	G	G	-	G	G	G	G	G	-	G	G	G	G	G	-	G	G
CON	CON 204	G	G	G	-	G	Y	G	G	G	-	G	Y	G	G	G	-	G	Y	G	G	G	-	G	Y	G	G	G	-	G	Y
CON	CON 210	G	G	G	-	G	G	G	G	G	-	G	G	G	G	G	-	G	G	G	G	G	-	G	G	G	G	G	-	G	G
CON	CON 232	-	-	-	-	-	-	G	G	G	-	G	G	G	G	G	-	G	G	G	G	G	-	G	G	G	G	G	-	G	G
CON	CON 234	G	G	G	-	G	G	G	G	G	-	G	G	G	G	G	-	G	G	G	G	G	-	G	G	G	G	G	G	-	G
CON	CON 235	G	G	Y	-	G	R	G	G	G	-	G	G	-	-	-	-	-	-	G	G	G	-	G	G	G	G	G	G	-	Y
CON	CON 236	-	-	G	Y	G	R	G	G	G	-	G	G	-	-	-	-	-	-	-	-	-	-	-	-	G	G	G	G	-	G
CON	CON 237	-	-	G	Y	G	G	-	-	G	G	G	G	-	-	G	G	G	G	-	-	G	Y	G	Y	-	-	G	G	G	G
CON	CON 243	G	G	G	-	G	G	G	G	G	-	G	G	G	G	G	-	G	G	G	G	G	-	G	G	G	G	G	-	G	G
CON	CON 244	G	G	G	-	G	G	G	G	G	-	G	G	G	G	G	-	G	G	G	G	G	-	G	G	G	G	G	-	G	G
CON	CON 250	G	G	G	-	G	G	G	G	G	-	G	G	G	G	G	-	G	G	-	-	-	-	-	-	G	G	G	-	G	G
CON	CON 251	-	-	-	-	-	-	G	G	G	-	G	G	G	G	G	-	G	G	-	-	-	-	-	-	G	G	G	-	G	G
CON	CON 260A	-	-	G	G	G	G	-	-	G	G	G	G	-	-	G	G	G	Y	-	-	G	G	G	G	-	-	G	G	G	G
CON	CON 260B	-	-	-	-	-	-	G	G	G	-	G	G	G	G	G	-	G	G	G	G	G	-	G	G	G	G	G	-	G	G
CON	CON 353	G	G	G	-	G	G	G	G	G	-	G	G	G	G	G	-	G	G	G	G	G	-	G	G	G	G	G	-	G	G
	GRT 201	G	R	G	-	G	G	-	-	-	-	-	-	G	G	G	-	G	G	G	R	G	-	G	G	G	G	G	-	G	G
	IND 100	-	-	-	-	-	-	G	G	G	-	G	G	G	G	G	-	G	G	-	-	-	-	-	-	G	G	G	-	G	G
	IND 103	G	-	G	R	G	G	G	-	G	Y	Y	G	-	-	-	-	-	-	G	-	G	R	G	G	G	-	G	R	G	G
	IND 200	-	-	-	-	-	-	G	G	G	-	G	G	G	G	G	-	G	G	-	-	-	-	-	-	G	G	G	-	G	G
	LAW 801	G	G	G	-	G	G	-	-	-	-	-	-	G	G	G	-	G	G	G	G	G	-	G	G	G	G	G	-	G	G

Instructor Category Scale: 5.25-5.99; Categories 2-6 Scale: 5.25-5.59;
Cat 2-Environ; Cat 3-Courseware; Cat 4-Online Delivery; Cat 5-Lrng Effectiveness; Cat 6-Job Impact

	1	2	3	4	FY
G	75	102	102	90	115
Y	6	7	3	3	4
R	4	1	0	2	1

	1	2	3	4	FY
G	88%	93%	97%	95%	96%
Y	7%	6%	3%	3%	3%
R	6%	1%	0%	2%	1%

Figure A4.5　DAU Efficiency and Effectiveness Scorecard

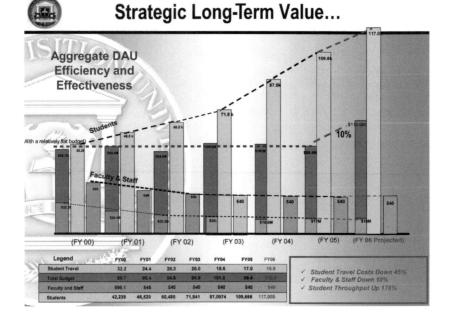

Cisco Sales Training

Cisco delivers a wide variety of talent-drive and performance-driven sales training through web-based courses, instructor-led training, and video on-demand. The company carefully tracks utilization and measures the impact of the talent-driven programs ("Sales Master Series") and initiative-based programs on sales results. You can see their volume metrics and impact measurement data in Figures A4.6 and A4.7.

The company measures "impact" by comparing sales of individuals who have attended courses versus those who did not. While this not a rigorous ROI, it gives Cisco a strong sense of what is working.

Microsoft Learning

Microsoft Learning is responsible for all external training and learning resellers. It records many important measures, derived from

Figure A4.6 Cisco Sales Training Volume Metrics

Sales force development measuring impact is key

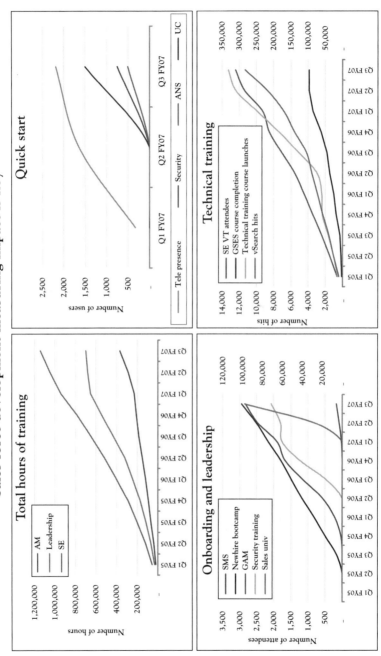

Figure A4.7 Cisco Sales Impact Measurement

Sales force development impact on sales growth

Impact Metrics

Analysis based on

Sales master series : 1620 AMs, 342 sales leaders

New hire field training : FY07 Q1/Q2 only, 888 New hires on sales plan

Security training initiative : 1272 attendees Participants overall: 56% decrease in attrition rate, 15.9% higher pipeline by revenue, and 9.8% increase in closed revenue

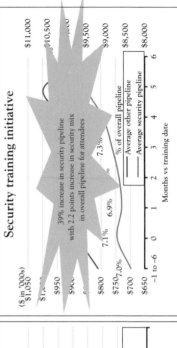

Security training initiative

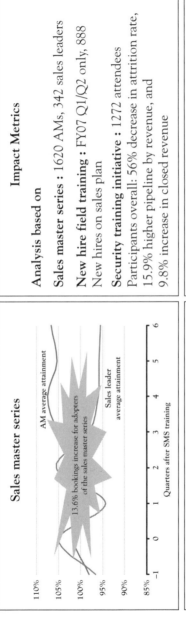

Sales master series

New hire field training

Source: Cisco, 2007

revenue, satisfaction, adoption, utilization, and impact. Much of its measurement focus also helps identify which learning providers are giving the highest quality and highest value learning to its customers. Their scorecard is shown in Figure A4.8.

Sprint University

Sprint University (now part of Sprint/Nextel) has developed a very mature model for delivering actionable information. It also uses KnowledgeAdvisors as its measurement and analytics system.

The Sprint University measurement team consists of nine employees in a total organization of three hundred. It uses standard evaluations, driven by KnowledgeAdvisors, with an approach that follows a three-tier model:

Short training programs, under one hour, are evaluated with a short-form Level 1 evaluation;

Medium-length programs (one to four hours), are evaluated with a long-form Level 1 evaluation; and

Long programs (more than four hours) are evaluated with a long-form evaluation, manager evaluations, and follow-up evaluations.

Sprint's biggest challenges today are integration of the KnowledgeAdvisors system with its Saba LMS and convincing line-of-business organizations to believe that satisfaction measures are important. Interestingly enough, 40 percent of Sprint University's clients are customer service and support representatives. These business units regularly use customer service as quality metrics. Yet, when the training organization shows similar metrics, they question the validity of the results. As described in the Six Sigma discussion earlier in this book, customer satisfaction (that is, attainment of customer objectives) is a critical measure and learning leaders must continue to explain its value to the organization. Some samples from Sprint University are shown in Figures A4.9 and A4.10.

Figure A4.8   Microsoft Learning Certification Scorecards

Microsoft Certified Professional Exams

1   Key trends

- Q2 FY06 NSAT inline with budget and FY05 total
- Q2 NSAT increased by 4 points versus Q1 FY06
- NSAT for Pass/Fail as subgroups increased slightly in FY06 versus FY05

NSAT	FY05	Q1 FY06	Q2 FY06	H1 FY06	Goal FY06	Variance Y/Y	Variance budget
Exams							

Fiscal year	Pass/Fail	NSAT	Evaluation count	% of total count
FY05	Fail			
	Pass			
FY06	Fail			
	Pass			

2   Title ranking

FY06 Top 3 Titles by NSAT(o=25) – Pass	FY05	Q1 FY06	Q2 FY06	H1 FY06	Change Y/Y
70-306: Developing and Implementing Web MSFT Win-based Apps					
70-305: Developing and Implementing Web Apps					
70-210: Installing, Configuring, and Administering Microsoft Windows 2000					

FY06 Bottom 3 Titles by NSAT(o=25) – Pass	FY05	Q1 FY06	Q2 FY06	H1 FY06	Change Y/Y
70-296: Planning, Implementing, Maintaining a WS03 Environment					
70-297: Designing a WS03 Active Directory and Network Infrastructure					
70-292: Managing and Maintaining a WS03 Environment					

3   Attribute ratings

Net Attribute Score (top 2 box – bottom 4 box) + 100	FY05	H1FY06	Change Y/Y
Exam registration process			
Test center quality			
Rigor of content			
Language quality			
Impact of passing exam: career potential			
Ease of finding training resources			
Appropriateness of question format			
Usefulness of score report			
Impact of exam prep: job effectiveness			
Relevancy of skills to job			
Ability of exam to test real problems			
Quality of training resources			
Clarity of questions			
Alignment training resources to exam			
Effectiveness of prep guide			

4   Satisfaction drivers (Pass)

Derived Importance

High Importance/High Satisfaction

High Importance/Low Satisfaction

Lower Importance/High Satisfaction

Lower Importance/Low Satisfaction

Ability of exam to test real-life problems

Clarity of exam questions

Relevancy of skills needed to type of job performed

Effectiveness of the Exam Prep Guide to prepare for this exam

Degree to which question format is appropriate for skills tested

Impact of passing the exam on career potential

Alignment of Microsoft training resources with the exam

Degree to which exam content ensures ongoing quality of MCPs

Usefulness of score report

% "Extraordinary/Outstanding" Rating

Figure A4.9 Sprint University Measurement Strategy

Metrics that "really" matter

- Written comments
  Managers, trainers and instructional designers

- Quick question report
  Managers, trainers and instructional designers

- Comparative performance reports
  Managers, trainers and instructional designers

- Human capital ROI card
  Senior executives, directors and training managers

- Report cards
  HRD scorecard

Figure A4.10 Sprint University Instructor Analysis

Comparative Performance Report*

Benchmark	# Evaluations	Avg Score
My Average	411	6.34

Instructors	# Evaluations	Avg Score
Instructor 21298	1	7.00
Instructor 20177	15	6.93
Instructor 20174	6	6.88
Instructor 15618	1	6.87
Instructor 15746	16	6.86
Instructor 20292	7	6.76
Instructor 20289	6	6.76
Instructor 22685	28	6.67
Instructor 20269	20	6.65
Instructor 20290	13	6.62
Instructor 20270	24	6.60
Instructor 20273	20	6.54
Instructor 20285	18	6.52
Instructor 20176	5	6.50
Instructor 20265	17	6.49
Instructor 20293	8	6.47
Instructor 20170	5	6.47

Specific Learning Measures

Figure A5.1 gives a number of examples of learning measures that can be used to capture information in some of the Bersin & Associates Impact Measurement Framework areas.

Figure A5.1 Sample Impact Framework Measures

Satisfaction	Adoption	Utility	Efficiency	Alignment	Attainment
Satisfaction with instructor, program materials, facility.	Total student-hours consumed.	Learner/manager perceived improvement in job productivity.	Total cost to develop.	Manager assessment of priority of program relative to other priorities.	Six Sigma quality measures against stated client objectives.
Satisfaction with program's execution against stated objectives.	% of audience who has enrolled, completed vs. target.	Learner/manager willingness to recommend the program.	Total cost to deliver.	Learner/manager perception of priority of this course vs. others.	Course delivered on-budget by %.
	Adoption by audience (i.e., manager, geography, business unit).	Improvement in performance plan measures after course.	Development cost per hour of instruction.	Manager assessment of program value relative to time investment.	Course delivered on-time by % or days.
	Total # of enrollments, completions.	Learner perceived relevance of this course to his/her current job.	Total cost (development and delivery) per student hour consumed.	Learner assessment of program value relative to time investment.	Quality (i.e., # of bugs, typos, errors) per hour of instruction.
		Measured change in root cause indicator from performance consulting.	Time to build, time to complete	Learner assessment of how well the program was supported by manager.	
		Financial return from signoff sheet multiplied by perceived % return.	Class, instructor, facility utilization rate.	How well were managers involved in the signoff process for the program?	
		Learner/manager perceived value of course to business return.	Course reuse ratio (# of hours used vs. hours in development).		
What is the average program satisfaction and how does it compare over time?	What is the aggregate percent of target adoption across the entire organization?			What percent of programs are considered "strategic" in the learning investment model?	What is the six-sigma measure of customer quality for this program vs. others?

Training Analytics Specifications

Introduction

After you have implemented a measurement program for several years, you will reach a point at which you want to use the data you are collecting for detailed reports and analysis. You will start to analyze measures by audience, program, geography, tenure with your company, and more. If you are a retailer, for example, you are likely to want to aggregate data by store, region, district, state, and country. Most LMS systems are not well equipped to create these reports. In this case, you probably want to specify or build an "analytics" application for your training data. This part of the book will help you—it is a "specification" you can use to help design or buy such a system.

It has been developed after more than five years of experience in the development, specification, and implementation of training measurement and analytics systems. We have consulted with more than thirty different companies on the development and implementation of such systems.

This section is designed as a set of general guidelines for buyers and vendors, to assist in the process of building or buying such systems.

1.0. Business Measures

In this section, we define which major business measures are important to the organization. These will typically fall into the nine categories in the impact model or, more broadly, into the categories of efficiency, effectiveness, and compliance. Before you specify a system, you should understand what measures you want to capture.

You can probably predict many of these in advance, but typically these measures are developed over several years of work in developing various reports for various purposes. Typical measures include the nine Impact Measurement measures, as well as those discussed in the following paragraphs.

1.1. Efficiency

Efficiency measures are used to measure training volumes, capacity utilization, and cost effectiveness:

- Volumes (enrollments, completions, student hours, percent complete, continuing education units);
- Utilization (instructor utilization, room utilization, course utilization, session utilization, where utilization is usually defined as number of hours used versus total number of hours available); and
- Financial (cost per student hour, cost per course, cost per session, cost of external supplies, cost of external content providers).

1.2. Effectiveness

Effectiveness measures cover data that helps to identify overall or relative effectiveness of a program, instructor, facility or the overall training organization:

- Completion rate (percent of students who complete);
- Scores (aggregate score or better, percent of mastery score, pass/fail);

- Satisfaction (Level 1 ratings, should be on standardized measures, the organization must determine whether a standard rating scale will be used and, if so, how it will be administered);

- Customer satisfaction (attainment) measures (which may include percent over budget, delivery on schedule, time to build, and time to deploy);

- Alignment measures (which may include level of signoff on program, indicators of manager adoption, and manager satisfaction measures); and

- Business impact (there are many ways to measure this, the simplest being satisfaction measures from first-line managers; other ways may include correlation with non-learning data. We recommend trying to compute ROI using an analytics system).

1.3. Compliance

Compliance measures are used to measure strict compliance with mandatory programs or certification programs. These measures tend to have special requirements.

Definition of Completion

- Will the compliance completion requirements have special needs? (For example, is "completion" defined as both completing the course and obtaining a minimum score?)

- Does completion include a passing score in three out of five modules?

- Does completion mean spending a certain amount of time?

These computations may not be supported by the LMS and should be "computable" in the analytics system.

Measuring Important Dates and Times. Some certifications must be completed by a certain date; if so, the following should be measured:

- Days to complete (days before a completion deadline is passed, after which the individual may have to restart);
- Days to expire (days before a person must "recertify" if he or she is already certified); and,
- Rolling windows (days after an event, for example, an individual must complete this certification within thirty days from his or her first day at work, or he or she must complete this certification within three months of promotion) and, therefore, "days to certify" based on these rolling windows.

Recertification Rules. If a certification is updated, all existing certifications may need to be recertified, so the system must show "days to recertify."

1.4. Business Data

What critical business data should correlate with learning data? This area can open up a lot of requirements, but the most important point to understand is that, in order to correlate learning data with business data (that is, sales revenues, percent of quota, error rate, time to complete a call, and so on), the "grain" of both pieces of data must be identical. For example, to have sales revenue by "sales rep" and by "month," then the training manager must be able to look at learning data by "sales rep" and by "month."

To import business data into the analytics system, the system must also support specific data types—revenues, percentages, days, minutes, and so on. It is important to write these data elements down and decide by priority how important they are to actually run in the same system, or whether they can be correlated and matched externally.

In most cases, this data is coming from a different system and will have to be extracted, transformed, and loaded (ETL = extract/transform/load) programs or tools to load the data into the analytics system. Many toolsets (Microsoft, for example) have ETL tools built in to simplify this process. In Chapter 6: Measurement of Business Impact, we discuss how you identify and find this data.

2.0. Dimensions

In any analytics system, information is grouped and sorted by "dimensions." A dimension, from an analytics standpoint, is some characteristic of the information to use for grouping, sorting, and aggregating.

Dimensions are hierarchical, meaning they form a tree. For example, in the "organizational dimension," the CEO is the top, the senior vice presidents are the first branch, and on down the line. At each level of the dimensional hierarchy, the analytics system automatically recomputes the measures that apply to that dimension. For example, for the total number of student hours consumed for a given course, at the CEO level results can be seen for the whole company. In "drilling" down to the senior vice president level, results will be seen for student hours for those in the senior vice president's organization (as well as the senior vice president's peers), and so on down the line. This hierarchical nature of dimensions and drilling functionality is one of the most powerful features of an analytics system, because it lets the user drill down to find anomalies in the data.

2.1. Basic Training Analytics Dimensions

From our experience in the design and implementation of measurement, the typical dimensions for analysis are:

- Organizational hierarchy (worker, manager, district manager, vice president, executive vice president, and so on);

- Course catalog (by course, by course group, by certification family);
- Delivery type (for all e-learning courses, for all live courses, for all books);
- By vendor (for all NETg courses, for all SkillSoft courses and so on);
- By geography (for all learners in California, for all learners in the western region);
- By functional area (for all salespeople, for all manufacturing engineers);
- By customer (for customer education, only one account should be viewed);
- By job class or skill level;
- By instructor (for review of instructor utilization); and
- By facility and by room (for analysis of room and facility utilization).

2.2. Organizing Employees (Hierarchies)

In most organizations, there are three different dimensional hierarchies for employees.

The "management hierarchy" organizes data according to who reports to whom. From the LMS standpoint, this is often the most important hierarchy, because it establishes how the manager will view the employees' training records. For actionable information, this is very valuable; it finds which managers need to take action if some training intervention requires attention. The challenge with this hierarchy is getting a reliable data feed that maintains it. Usually this information is stored in the HR system (SAP or Oracle's PeopleSoft) and can be fed into the analytics system in a daily or weekly batch.

The "organizational hierarchy" organizes data according to your employees' respective business units. In most organizations, this is different and distinct from the management hierarchy. For example, at Cisco, an employee may be part of the "home router" business unit, which reports into the "router group," which reports into the "products division," which reports into "manufacturing." This hierarchy is often identified by the employee's organization code, also stored in the HR system. It is very valuable for financial analysis; for example: "How much training did the manufacturing division consume?" or "How much should we recharge them for the SkillSoft catalog?"

The "geographic hierarchy" organizes people by location. In most HR systems, people have a "location code," which indicates where they work. Again, this is often independent of the other two hierarchies. There could be salespeople located in a manufacturing location, for example. The value of the geographic hierarchy is to identify trends in training that may be cultural or location-specific. For example, why is it that all the attendees in the Hawaii education center come from the eastern United States in the winter? Why do German employees avoid taking the compliance course?

To simplify the implementation, it is best to choose one first, but an analytics system can easily support all three. The only issue is to make sure the organization has a reliable source of information for these dimensions so that they can stay up-to-date.

2.3. Time Dimension

In an analytics system, all reports have a time window. These should be flexible and easy to use; examples are "year to date," "this year versus last year at this time," "this quarter," "summarized by quarter for the last six quarters," and many more. The organization should define which date ranges are used in existing reports and make sure the product/system supports these with a minimum of setup.

The "time dimension" is also hierarchical, for example: "I want to see a metric by month, then aggregate it by quarter and then aggregate by year." The key issue here is defining how to define "start and end time." If a course started on 6/30 and finished on 7/15, does it go into Q2 or Q3? These decisions have to be made when the ETL scripts are set up to load data.

3.0. Hierarchy and Aggregation

The big difference between a true analytics system and an SQL-based reporting system is the ability to dynamically drill up and down the hierarchy and to aggregate data. For example, in a true analytics system, the training manager should be able to do the following without any special reports:

Drilling. Compute the number of enrollments in a given course over this year for, say, nine states in the western area. Now, theoretically speaking, drill down and see the number of enrollments by state for each of the nine states. Then drill down into one state and see the enrollments by manager. Drill down further into that manager and see enrollment list by student.

Sorting. When drilling down into the nine states, the training manager might want to sort the states from high to low. When drilling down into the managers within a state, he or she might only want to see the top ten managers (there may be hundreds).

Filtering. While drilling, the training manager may want to change the dimensions or filters. In this example, drilling down into the nine states to see that California's enrollments seem low, he or she may want to look at enrollments in more than one course to see whether there is a trend among all courses in California. Or, drilling down into California and seeing low enrollments, the training manager may want to filter the data by e-learning only to see whether this group is taking more e-learning and less instructor-led training than other states.

4.0. Computational Flexibility

With an analytics system, there are many computations to make to turn numbers into more actionable information. For example, total number of enrollments may not be useful, whereas enrollment rate[1] may be very useful. Completion rate would be a similar computation.

Analytics systems should allow the flexibility to take a "measure" as defined above and create a "computed measure," which is that measure divided by or multiplied by some other measure. In general, the most common computation would be to take some learning metric and divide it by the total number of people eligible or working in that group. This is in order to take measures like "enrollments, completions, and cost" and compute "enrollment rate, completion rate, and cost per enrollment."

A "**computed measure**" is that measure divided by or multiplied by some other measure.

5.0. Security and Roles

5.1. Security

It is important to consider who needs the information in the analytics system and make sure the information is only available to those who need it. Some examples of typical security rules include the following:

- No one in the organization may see any information from organizations above him or her in the hierarchy;
- No one in the organization can see information from any organization outside of his or her business unit, unless he or she is above some level in the hierarchy; and
- No one in the organization can see financial information unless he or she is an administrator.

5.2. Roles

Roles are used to create and administer these security rules. The typical types of roles created are:

- **Analysts.** People who can view all the information and are typically in training analyst roles;

- **First-line managers/directors.** People who can see their workgroups or their organizations only;
- **Executives.** People who can see all the workgroups under them, but may not need to or want to have access to drilling into individual workgroups; and
- **Training managers.** People who, like administrators, can see financial information about the efficiency and cost-effectiveness of the training organization.

6.0. Dashboards

The term "dashboard" refers to the system's ability to create customized, easy-to-view web pages or reports that have aggregated information that is set up in advance. A training manager may want to create a dashboard that shows "western area sales completion rate for new hire certification by state" and run it every two weeks, and make this a dashboard for the western area sales vice president. These dashboards may have multiple measures on them and often have graphs to make them easy to use.

The system should be able to create these easily without a lot of custom programming; otherwise, many information consumers will never bother to learn how to use the system to run the reports.

Another important feature in most analytics systems is the ability to create charts. A bar chart showing completion rate by business unit is far more valuable than a series of numbers in a table. Charts that have "target metrics" are usually called dashboards; for example, if the target "cost per enrollment" is $175, the training manager should be able to see the cost per enrollment for each program and a red or green bar showing how much above or below $175 each program is.

7.0. Alerts and Report Subscriptions

An important add-on to dashboards is the ability for the system to send "alerts" and "subscriptions" to important reports and dashboards. For example, "If the completion rate is below 75 percent for new hire training, send a report to each manager every week" or "If the new hire certification failure rate is greater than 10 percent, send a report to the first-line manager."

Subscriptions simply allow people to receive similar reports on a regular basis. The training manager may want each district manager to see the enrollment rates for their regional store managers once per quarter or once per month. Once this report is set up, the system should be able to send it to this group automatically.

8.0. Extract, Transform, and Load

In order for an analytics system to be useful and actionable, the information in the system must be accurate and up-to-date. This requires that all information about learning programs, learners, management hierarchies, locations, and financial cost and price must be current and correct. How does this occur? The process is called "ETL" or extract, transform, and load, as previously mentioned.

Typically in such a system, the data in the analytics system is coming from the LMS—in some cases the learning data may come from the LMS, and other data may come from the HR or sales or other business system. The ETL process is a very critical process that takes all the "system of record" information and moves it into the LMS and analytics system, so that it is accurate and current. The analytics system must have ETL "tools," which make it easy to build and maintain these SQL scripts that load this information. If these scripts are built by hand, the process will be costly, error-prone, and very difficult to maintain.

The buyer must identify where the **"source of truth"** is for all this information. Is the actual corporate hierarchy stored in Oracle's PeopleSoft or another HR system? Or does it come from the financial system? The training manager will need to know this, so that the LMS has accurate and current information. Also ask the vendors what tools, if any, they have to ensure data quality. Can data types and rules be enforced (for example, all course names have capital first letters or all scores be between 1 and 100)? If these rules are not created and enforced, the analytics system will produce faulty results and aggregations will not work correctly.

9.0. General

Analytics systems should make it easy to export data into Microsoft Excel, Adobe PDF, or other Microsoft Office formats, so it is easy to build presentations and reports and do further analysis on the data.

10.0. Creating Demonstration Scripts

After considering the issues above and incorporating these into the requirements, it is important to ask the vendors to give a demonstration of the system with actual live data. A typical demonstration script may look like this.

10.1. General Analytics Functionality

"We have a four-level field organization with four employees per store and one manager. Every ten stores reports to a district manager, and every five district managers report to an area vice president. We would like to look at average enrollment rates for one course by store, by district, and at the area vice president level. We would also like to look at scores for this course: the average score by store, by district, and at the vice president level. Finally, when we drill down to the store level, we'd like to have a report generated that shows each learner, his or her name, his or her date of enrollment, date of completion, and score obtained."

10.2. Dashboard

"We have decided for this particular course that a 'passing score' is 75 or higher (on a 1 to 100 scale). We would like to set a threshold that says that any store or district that does not have an average passing score creates an alert. How would you create a dashboard at the area vice president level and at the district level that highlights those stores and districts that are out of compliance? And how would a district manager or vice president drill down to see the individual stores and individual employees who have failed to meet this criterion?"

10.3. Alerts

"For the example above, we would like to ask the system to send an email once per week for every district that has stores below the 75 percent passing threshold. And this email should have a list of the stores falling below the threshold, the names of the managers, and the names of the learners who did not pass. How would we set this up, and what would the email or report look like?"

10.4. Computed Measures

"How can we create a report that shows 'days to expire' for a certification where the 'days to expire' is defined as Alternative 1: 'days to expire' is the number of days before June 30 that a certification must be completed; Alternative 2: 'days to expire' is the number of days from the start of a certification for exactly six months that the certification must be completed; Alternative 3: 'days to expire' is the number of days from forty-five days from date of hire that a certification must be completed."

Note

1. Enrollment "rate" would be defined as the number of enrollments divided by the total number of learners eligible for enrollment.

Index

A

Actionable information
averages as failing to deliver, 17–20
consistent element of, 16–17
converting ROI analysis into, 48–50
credible element of, 17
defining, 15–17
on effectiveness, design, efficiency and effectiveness, 14
on larger talent challenges, 15
of LMS (learning management systems), 31
measurement focus on gathering, 179
as purpose of measurements, 13–14
specific element of, 15–16
on training compliance, 15
See also Information
Adoption measure, 91–92, 103*fig*, 104*fig*
Alignment. *See* Business alignment
Assessment. *See* Performance assessment
ASTD (American Society of Training and Development), 37
AT&T Wireless, 33
Attainment of client objectives measure. *See* Customer satisfaction measures
Audience analysis, 65
Audience targeting, 96
Averages
cautions when using, 17
examining learner satisfaction, 18*fig*–20
Aviation Industry, 32

B

Bersin, J., 61
Bersin model. *See* Impact Measurement Framework

Bersin research. *See* High Impact Learning Organization research
The Blended Learning Book, 96
Brinkerhoff, R., 68
Business
actionable information value to, 13–20, 48–50, 179
measuring training impact on, 140*fig*–151
performance improvement of, 13–14, 82–87, 103*fig*, 127–129, 128*fig*
training as support function of, 22–26, 23*fig*, 180*fig*
See also Business problems; Learning business plan; Organizations
Business alignment
Caterpillar's Planning and Budgeting Process example of, 154–156
challenge of developing, 153–154
CNA Insurance Training Investment model on, 156*fig*–157, 158*fig*
High Impact research on developing, 154
of highest ROI programs with urgent business problems, 53
Kirkpatrick model's lack of, 66
of learning objectives with, 24*fig*
managers on critical challenge of, 153
as organizational performance factor, 82–84
performance consulting to establish, 65, 75–76, 110–112
problem-definition phase and process of, 74–75
See also Alignment
Business alignment measures
Business Impact Model on, 82–84, 103*fig*, 104*fig*

249

Utility measure
  differentiating between performance
    and, 93
  Impact Measurement Framework,
    92–93, 103fig, 104fig
Utilization measures, 105

V

"Voice of the Customer," 68, 163, 166
  See also Customer satisfaction measures
Volume measure, 105

W

WhatWorks research, 3
  See also High Impact Learning Organi-
    zation research

Z

Zeroed-In Technologies, 175
Zoomerang, 172

About the Author

Josh Bersin is the CEO of Bersin & Associates, a well-known global research firm focused on enterprise learning and talent management. Mr. Bersin's research and consulting include in-depth studies and best-practice research with more than 450 global corporations, government, and non-profit institutions.

Mr. Bersin is also the author of *The Blended Learning Book*, (Pfeiffer, 2004), an authoritative and comprehensive study of e-learning and best practices in technology-based training, *The High-Impact Learning Organization* (Bersin & Associates, 2006), and *High-Impact Talent Management* (Bersin & Associates, 2007). His experience, focus, and innovative research focus on finding unique and practical ways to apply training and HR solutions to solve specific business challenges.

Mr. Bersin's professional experience includes ten years at IBM and seven years at Sybase Inc. He is the founder of two companies (Arista Knowledge Systems and Bersin & Associates) and has participated in executive leadership at DigitalThink. He has a bachelor's degree in mechanical engineering from Cornell, a master's in mechanical engineering from Stanford University, and an MBA from the University of California at Berkeley.

What will you find on pfeiffer.com?

- The best in workplace performance solutions for training and HR professionals

- Downloadable training tools, exercises, and content

- Web-exclusive offers

- Training tips, articles, and news

- Seamless on-line ordering

- Author guidelines, information on becoming a Pfeiffer Affiliate, and much more

Discover more at www.pfeiffer.com